DAUGHTER OF THE
Noble Orphan

A Memoir

RUBY Y. PRUETT

BLUEPRINT PRESS
INTERNATIONALE

ISBN
978-1-961117-41-9 (Paperback)
978-1-961117-42-6 (eBook)
978-1-961117-40-2 (Hardcover)

DAUGHTER OF THE
Noble Orphan

TABLE OF CONTENTS

FOREWORD

Growing up as a homeless orphan, Mother never had the opportunity to attend school beyond a few weeks in fourth grade. My father cared nothing for education, but Mother often said to him that she wanted her children to receive an education and "amount to something." Still, if what Robin Hood said his father taught him is true – nobility is determined not by birth or wealth but by one's actions – Mother became a noble person. She survived all manner of adversity, including flood, pain, poverty, and abandonment, but remained a virtuous woman, who contributed not only to her family but to everyone whose path crossed hers. She was my idol, and she exercised a far greater influence on my life than any other person. I consider her character a truly sterling one and worthy of remembering. Mother died in 1991; soon afterward I wrote a representative summary of her life, entitled *The Noble Orphan*, gleaned from notes I collected from my many interviews with her during the latter part of her life; hence, the title of my own story honors her memory.

Upon hearing some of the events of my life, many people have encouraged me to pen the entire story; until recently, I never gave any serious thought of undertaking such an enormous long-term project. Inwardly I questioned whether the story would be interesting enough to merit others' attention. In addition, I have remained absorbed in work of one kind or another since I was first sent to the cotton and corn fields of West Tennessee as a "farm hand" at age five – this in addition to helping Mother with gardening, canning, sewing, and a multitude of other chores when field work was done. I have never experienced the luxury of idleness, nor have I desired it.

In recent years in particular, several relatives and acquaintances have urged me to commit to such a work, assuring me my life is deserving of a permanent record also. Now in the beginning years of my ninth decade, I recognize my time left on earth is short, so finally I have reluctantly attempted to pen many events which are meaningful to me, some major and others minor. It has been pleasurable to recall and record the positive events, and painful to relate the negative ones. But I would be less than honest if I omitted them, because both kinds have influenced and shaped my character. All events are true, unless my memory has failed me, though I have changed names of some persons and organizations involved, owing to the intimacy of the subject matter.

My prayer is that those who read my story will find it instructive, and perhaps a little entertaining. I shall feel rewarded if it influences any reader's character positively and helps him/her to know the value of an education and hard work in reaching goals in life, in combination with a constant and strong faith in God.

Ruby Y. Pruett
December 2017

THE FAMILY I INHERITED

My beginning was neither auspicious nor promising. Mother wept bitterly when she discovered she was again with child. Since childhood, her life had been filled with hardships, loneliness, and poverty. After struggling almost seven years as a homeless orphan, she married my father, a widower twenty-four years her senior and father of seven children, who – unbeknownst to Mother at the time of their marriage – had just lost his home and farm.

She reared six of her seven stepchildren. In addition, she bore five surviving children of her own and suffered two miscarriages. At age 33, she was already aged and faded and was keenly aware she had little or no means of caring for another addition to her extended family. The entire country was in the midst of the Great Depression, but that does not explain all her circumstances. However, the following brief history of the family I was born into will make the reader understand her plight.

Mother, Novie Datha Cantrell, was born March 17, 1901, the fifth of 10 children, to William Alexander and Appalona Brewington Cantrell in rural Graves County, Kentucky. As long as her family was intact, she had a happy home life, for Grandfather Cantrell loved his family and made a sufficient living for them. Her brothers helped their father with the outside work of raising corn, tobacco, and wheat on their farm, in addition to helping to operate the family's grist mill and saw mill, while the girls helped their mother with household chores. However, her life was devastated when both parents died in 1911, shortly after her 10th birthday. She was separated permanently from her siblings thereafter and lived wherever she could find refuge, working as a cook, housekeeper, field hand, and nurse to "earn her board and keep" just as James Whitcomb Riley's "Little Orphant Annie" had to do.

Unfortunately, Mother's parents died intestate, and one of Grandmother Cantrell's relatives became executor of their estate. The orphaned children were left poor when everything was settled. Once, when Mother stayed in the executor's home a few weeks while he was searching for another home for her, he required Mother to work in the tobacco fields without pay while he deducted board at $1 a day from the Cantrell estate. When he "settled accounts" with the orphaned children – after having sold the house and farm, including all household goods, and farm implements – each child received about $20.

In only a few of the 12 homes in which Mother lived from age 10 until her marriage to my father in November 1917, was she treated kindly. She lived first with her maternal grandmother, Calvernia Wray Brewington, and step-grandfather, Sanford Dublin. Grandmother Dublin abused Mother verbally by making false accusations against her and administered other punishment. One time, an aunt who was caring for Mother's infant sister, Lona, came over for a visit. After dinner Mother stopped washing the dinner dishes long enough to kiss little Lona, who was sitting on the kitchen floor, playing. For this act of sisterly love, Grandmother Dublin struck her and ordered her to get back to her dishwashing!

As Mother blossomed into a beautiful teenager, a relative suggested she go to Memphis, where her seemly looks could earn her a good living on the streets! Two different men attempted to seduce her on more than one occasion. Each time this happened, Mother refused their advances, but quietly took her leave of the family as soon as she could find another dwelling place.

During the fall of 1917 both Mother and her younger sister, Nona, were looking for another place to live. Through some family contact, they learned the Jess Meadows family, who lived outside Kenton, Tennessee, was in need of additional cotton pickers. Arrangements were made for the girls to travel by train from Fulton, Kentucky, to Kenton, where a member of the Meadows family met them. Though the Meadows family was large, the work hard, and resources scarce, Mother and Nona were treated with nothing but love and respect by the entire family.

Neither Mother nor Nona had ever seen a cotton field before, much less picked cotton! They were not the ideal hired hands, but they received their small earnings just the same, in addition to room and board. The girls were soon told they could make their home with the Meadowses as long as they wished to do so, an offer which previously had never been made by relatives or anyone else.

During the cotton-picking season, Mr. and Mrs. Meadows went to see a Ballie Taylor Yates, in neighboring Gibson County, to discuss the possibility of renting farm land from him. The Meadowses were unable to rent land (the reason for which will be made clear later), but Mr. Yates told them he was looking for another caregiver and housekeeper for his seven children. He would pay $5 a week, the same amount he was currently paying a neighbor woman. (Rumor had it Widower Yates was no match for caregiver's temper and he was afraid of her!) The Meadowses recommended the Cantrell sisters, suggesting the $5 weekly wage could be split between the two young women.

Mr. Yates was sufficiently interested to pursue the matter, so he paid the Meadowses a few visits to enable him to look Mother and Nona over. After some discussions with the Meadowses and a few conversations with Mother, Mr. Yates proposed marriage to her, confessing later he knew having two unmarried teenage girls living in his house would give rise to scandal.

The Meadowses objected to the marriage, for they had heard Mr. Yates was a heavy drinker – and that he was a brawler when he was drunk. However, both Mother and Nona needed a permanent home. Also, Mother felt compassion for the Yates children, who were growing up without a mother. She remembered how uprooted and lonely her life had been since she had lost her parents, and she wished to help them.

She consented to marry Mr. Yates…with two stipulations: He must quit drinking altogether and permit Nona to live with the Yates family as long as she needed a home. Mr. Yates agreed to both conditions.

Little did Mother divine what challenges lay ahead! All the skills she had learned earlier would be tested through famine, flood, poverty, sickness, and eventually abandonment, after a brief marriage to a second husband, five years after Daddy's sudden death.

There was no hint of romance or love in the marriage. It was for practical reasons from both sides. Prior to their marriage Daddy had never kissed Mother, and the kisses were few following it. She had never spent any time alone with him, with one exception; Daddy had come along the lane leading from the main road to the Meadows' house, from which Mother was returning after fetching the Meadows' mail. Mother climbed into his wagon and rode the rest of the way home with him.

When Mr. Yates came for Mother on that crisp morning of November 2, 1917, to be married in a civil ceremony in Trenton in the adjoining county of Gibson, Nona was unable to accompany them, for she lay in bed recovering from an ugly knee injury owing to a fall from the cotton wagon. Nona knew she was to make her home with the Yates family; she also knew marriage would change her and Mother's relationship permanently, so she cried and clung so tightly to Mother when the couple left that bruises appeared on both Mother's arms.

After a wedding dinner with one of Mother's maternal uncle's family and spending the night there, Daddy brought Mother to his large rambling farm house. Thus, began their life together.

* * *

Daddy had not told Mother of the recent loss of his farm – or that the family must vacate the property by January 1 the following year. Nor would Daddy discuss the matter with Mother when she learned the facts from one of the neighbors soon after the marriage: In a drunken brawl Daddy had threatened the life of a neighbor who brought charges against him. In order for Daddy to avoid a jail sentence and have the charges dropped, he agreed to pay a specified amount of money or give the litigant his farm to meet that obligation. Obviously, he didn't have the money, so he was forced to give up his house and farm.

The Yates family vacated their property on January 1, 1918. Daddy never again made any effort to own property. Until his death in 1946, they were tenant farmers/sharecroppers; that is, the family lived on land owned by another and divided the annual crop yields on a basis agreed upon by both parties. They farmed land at several locations in West Tennessee counties during the ensuing years.

Daddy never divided the $5 weekly wage between Mother and Nona, nor did he seek medical help for Mother, who became quite ill for many weeks with the same kind of influenza that plagued the entire Western world during the winter of 1917-18, consequently taking many lives. The lengthy illness left Mother almost totally deaf.

Nor did Daddy keep for long his promise of sobriety. He came home drunk and wild after only a few weeks of marriage and was never able thereafter to control that acquired habit. He eventually abandoned all responsibility and depended on the family's meager earnings from tenant farming to sustain his wasteful and wayward lifestyle. Besides pocketing all the profit from the cotton crop, if they earned extra money from picking cotton for a neighbor or from selling game or hides, he took that too. He was verbally and physically abusive toward his family. One time he came home in a drunken stupor, lined the children up, took his gun, and threatened violence. Providentially, just then a neighbor came in and managed to wrest the gun from him.

Mother never complained but bore her lot quietly and became the real head of the family. She served as peacemaker during Daddy's drunken rages, and at all other times. She was always home caring for the family while Daddy was away spending the family's earnings on riotous living. She was (silently) particularly careful to protect us daughters and wouldn't leave us alone with Daddy if she could help it, though she taught us never to be disobedient or disrespectful toward him. I could never bring myself to tell Mother about how Daddy molested me; nor could I mention it to anyone else until I was past 50 years old.

It was owing to Mother's buoyant spirit and resourcefulness that the family survived intact. She was a tireless worker, day in and day out, and she became a loving caregiver for her stepchildren and many other extended family members who made their home there. In addition, there was always one field hand who made his home with the family. Among the things required of her were cooking and cleaning daily for the entire household; washing clothing, using only a scrub board; and fashioning the children's clothes from flour sacks, used clothing, or any scraps of material that came into her hands. She took the children on picnics in the woods any time she could, and she played games with them.

Also, she became both doctor and nurse when they were ill and, in time, became noted for her nursing skills. She cared for nine mothers and their infants who were born in our house, in addition to her own.

The neighbors learned that Mother could ease headaches or back pain with her rubbing techniques, so the words, "Send for Mrs. Yates" were frequently heard when they were experiencing pain. Two Dyer County physicians – Drs. David Wright of Trimble, and DeWitt Holland of Newbern – sent for her whenever there were infant deliveries in the Yates' neighborhood or a surrounding one. Sometimes Mother arrived on the scene prior to the doctor and had already performed the delivery by the time the doctor arrived.

Of necessity, Mother was a strict disciplinarian. With Daddy's permission, she disciplined her stepchildren as well as her own, for any infraction of her rules of behavior. She insisted on hard work and honesty at all times, and taught other moral principles, though there was no Bible or other reading material in our home for many years. Mother spoke of adultery so often I thought it must be the sin against the Holy Spirit! She taught the children always to do without what they could not afford, but to be happy when others prospered, and never to beg or accept charity. She insisted on proper table manners to the best of her ability. She forbade the children to talk about their unfortunate home life, lifting her right index finger to her lips any time they left the house. She valued education and insisted Daddy permit the children to attend school, though he cared little for formal learning and often made them skip school to work in the fields.

Is it any wonder Mother wept when she learned she was expecting me? She confessed later, however, I was such a contented, happy baby and brought her so much joy, she soon repented of those earlier misgivings.

BIRTH AND EARLY CHILDHOOD (1933-47)

The Yates family lived in the community of Poplar Ridge, on the Obion-Dyer County Line Road, three miles west of Trimble, Tennessee, from 1930-47 and farmed 100 acres of land owned by a country gentleman, Mr. Herbert Morris of Obion. They grew cotton, corn, and soybeans, but cotton was the main cash crop. My brother, Morris Horton, and I – Mother and Daddy's last two children – were born in the old four-room tenant farmhouse there. Part of Horton's name honored our landlord.

Doctor David Wright delivered me at home on the chilly morning of November 21, 1933. The family was so poor Mother never owned a diaper for me, nor any other infant clothing. She pinned strips of old worn sheets and flour sacks on me and kept me covered with ragged quilts she had stitched earlier by hand. I still have a copy of the only picture taken of me as an infant. I was sitting alone, naked – except for a rag pinned around the lower part of my body - see front cover of the book. I remember sleeping in an old dilapidated cradle until I grew so big my feet dangled out one end where the spindles were missing.

The Great Depression was in full sway during the 1930s. Hardships and deprivations persisted for years, but our family had been impoverished long before, and for many years afterward. Many people received financial assistance from the Federal Government during President Roosevelt's administration, but Mother steadfastly refused to make application for any support. She had not read James Montgomery's works, but she espoused his philosophy, "I was not born, I have not lived, I shall not die… a parasite." She believed firmly in self-reliance, practiced it, and taught it to her children.

Instead of depending on the government, Mother doubled her efforts to eke out a living for her dependents by raising bigger gardens and more poultry products, so she could barter or sell any extra chickens, eggs or farm produce. She also sold milk, butter, and cream when those products could be spared. During those lean years, we often had little more to eat than field peas, and cornbread. Mother sometimes bartered peas and other vegetables and fouls for basic necessities.

* * *

I remember little of the first few years of my life. There are two incidents Mother enjoyed telling about me as a toddler. One was the time she brought me to the garden with her when I was just beginning to talk. I was immediately attracted to the fluted squash which were similar in color, shape, and size to the ancient sugar bowl – also fluted - that remained always on our kitchen table – covered between meals – and I babbled to Mother, "Mama, look to duh sushy bowls!" The other incident occurred when Mother had just finished scrubbing the wooden kitchen floor (with the cleanest tub of water left from her weekly laundry) and told me to shut the back door, which opened onto the back porch, to keep anyone from entering, stamping dirty footprints on the clean floor while it was still wet. I sat playing and did not obey her promptly. For that delay, I received a spanking. Shortly thereafter, someone opened the door again and failed to close it, so Mother again instructed me to go shut the door. This time I quickly responded, "In a minute, Mama, no, no spank de bobba."

Though only four years old, I still have a vague memory of seeing water everywhere when the Mississippi River overflowed its banks in early 1937, as well as the Obion River, one of her tributaries, forcing many families, including ours, to evacuate. Fortunately, Mother realized the flood would reach our area and made preparations the best she could. She spent an entire day emptying our "storm house," an earthen dugout in our front yard, of almost 1,000 jars of canned goods the day before the floodwaters reached our house. After the cows and mules had been taken to higher ground and the hogs and chickens placed in the loft of our barn, we were taken in small boats to the Poplar Ridge schoolhouse, which stood on the highest hill in the area, where we remained with four other families until the flood waters receded.

Mother prepared meals for all five families during our entire stay in the schoolhouse. The Red Cross set up a temporary supply station at Kenton, and men brought food and other necessities to the evacuees in boats. The experience made such an indelible impression on Mother that she spoke of the Flood of '37 the remainder of her life.

CHILD WORKER

From an early age Mother and I formed a strong lifelong bond. Besides the tenderness and love she showed me, and my complete admiration for her, there were practical reasons for our closeness: I was an obedient child, and she knew she could depend on me as her helper; and I was a willing interpreter, compensating for her deafness.

As a youngster, my work included various tasks. Some were annual, some seasonal, but many were daily chores. I brought in wood for the kitchen stove year-round and wood for the fireplace in winter. I helped Mother wash and hang out clothes and bring them inside when they were dry. When we finally purchased a gas-powered washing machine, I once caught my right arm in the wringer; it flattened my arm before Mother could stop the machine, but it soon returned to its normal shape. I helped Mother feed her chickens and gather eggs. I plucked chickens regularly for Mother to fry or to cook and use with dressing for our Sunday dinners. I helped with the gardening and canning, including hominy and kraut making. I sewed and stuffed sacks of sausage at hog-killing time and helped render lard from the swines' fat portions (leaving the delicious-tasting cracklin's Mother would add to cornbread batter), and make lye soap from recycled hog fat, a practice I still continue to do. I primed the well pump and pumped buckets of water for household use and filled a huge hollow log each day for the barnyard animals.

In addition, I shucked dried corn and, using a corn sheller, shelled a box full daily for the farm animals. Once, when my brother, Wade, and his family came from Nashville for a visit, his daughter, Peggy Joyce, only a few months younger than I, accompanied me to the barn to help shell the corn.

When we were finished and returned to the house, Peggy Joyce eagerly announced to the family, "I helped Ruby pull feathers from the corn!"

She had earlier informed me that city girls were "smarter" than country girls, so I knew she must be speaking the truth; still, I was mighty puzzled when she identified the corn shucks as feathers.

Our family never grew strawberries, but Mr. Olan Page, a truck farmer of the Mason Hall community, a few miles east of Trimble, raised multiple fields of the plump, sweet berries for commercial purposes. Each spring when the berries began to ripen, Mr. Page drove his truck down our road and hauled pickers to his fields each day throughout the season. Several in our family were his regular hands. We picked some of the fields one day and the remaining ones the next, so all the berries were gathered every two days. They were shipped by rail nightly to Chicago and were on the market the following morning.

As with cotton, I became a champion picker. At the height of the season, I could pick 100 quarts a day! Paid two cents per quart, earning $2 in one day seemed to me almost a fortune!

At the end of the season, when the berries were too small for profitable commercial purposes, Mr. Page allowed his hired hands to pick all they needed for their family. At that time, we would spend the entire day picking those small, ripe berries and bring them home for Mother to can after we had eaten fresh ones to our fill.

Another spring/summer job was picking blackberries which grew profusely in our woods. The spikes of the vines on which they grew contained briars; they were not as gentle on the hands as picking strawberries. Still, our family picked many gallons each year to be canned. Mother sometimes tied a gallon bucket around my waist and sent me to pick berries by myself, instructing me not to return home until my bucket was full. Though I obeyed, I was never eager to go into the woods alone.

Also, what we called scaly-bark hickory nuts and black walnuts grew plentifully in the Obion River woods. We drove a wagon to the woods each fall and filled it with these nuts. They required hulling, cleaning, and then spreading out to dry for a few weeks before cracking and picking out those rich, delicious nut meats. We ate them for snacks, and Mother used them for making candy and baking cakes around Christmas time.

Mother often sat at her machine for hours, sewing for the family, neighbors, and anyone else who asked for her help. When her back began to ache, she asked me to work the treadle for her, allowing her back to rest by changing positions. I would sit on the floor at the back of the machine and work the treadle until my little back ached, too.

Though Mother could be made to understand in a conversation one on one if the person spoke loudly, her influenza-caused deafness left her unable to distinguish sounds in a crowd where several voices were speaking simultaneously. Greatly handicapped by her hearing impairment, she struggled with the problem for many years. As soon as I was old enough, I became willing to yell any message into her ears until she understood it. Mother often referred to me as her buddy, "Ruby Doll." That moniker embarrassed me as I grew up, for I realized my siblings resented it. It is a precious memory to me now. Eventually, she was able to purchase a crude hearing device, but it was never a satisfactory solution.

Many years later, when Mother was in her 50s, she learned of a Shea Hearing Clinic in Memphis, reputed to be able to restore hearing for many people. Mother made arrangements to visit there. One of the Drs. Shea performed surgery on each of her ears to remove scar tissue on her eardrums, and her hearing was restored almost to perfection. It was a miracle for her, and she remained under Dr. Shea's care for the remainder of her life and spoke of him as a family friend.

After the "miraculous" restoration of Mother's hearing, she once called me "Loud Mouth" and wondered why I couldn't speak in a quieter tone of voice. That appellation hurt my feelings deeply, but I said nothing – and I doubt whether Mother ever realized my strong, loud voice was the result of all those years of yelling into her ears.

Besides becoming Mother's constant helper, Daddy assigned me work also. From an early age he sent me to the field each spring to hoe/chop cotton and corn, a job that lasted several weeks, for there were several fields, and each one was hoed twice before being plowed a final time and laid by. I hoed a row up and down the field just as the adults did.

Our landlord would occasionally bring his young blind son, Herbert Morris, Jr. (Mrs. Morris was also blind but a gifted pianist.), to the field where we were working, holding "Baby Herbert," as we called him, by the hand. We were always excited to see them and deferred to young man's every wish.

Cotton was harvested in the fall. Hand picking cotton was a backbreaking and laborious chore that often required several weeks' work, as there were sometimes three pickings of each field to ensure every boll was gathered as it matured.

When I was five, Daddy sent me to the cotton field as a regular hand. The only difference was that in the beginning I "carried" (picked) only one row at a time and was expected to keep pace with the adults, who carried two rows each. Mother fashioned my first cotton sack from a 100-pound feed sack, to which she sewed a rag strap to fit over my shoulder. As I became an accomplished picker, I graduated to five-foot sacks and still later to seven-foot ones, made of heavy cotton duck material.

As each cotton boll matured, it opened to reveal its four or five burs with fluffy locks of cotton bursting forth between each one. The leaves surrounding the unripe cotton boll and twigs from the end of the branches of the stalks would dry and become brittle; sometimes these bits of debris clung to the fluffy cotton locks, instead of crumbling and falling to the ground. Some of the pickers were careless and made no effort to remove them. As a result, their sacks often contained trash, producing a heavier poundage but inferior cotton quality, for the debris must be removed in the ginning process; whereas, cleaner cotton yielded more weight when deseeded and brought a higher price. I quickly became quite adept as a clean cotton picker, just as Daddy demanded of his family.

Another problem was what was called goose picking; that is, leaving bits of cotton in the boll; that was considered a great waste. Not only did I remove any debris from the cotton locks before placing them in my sack, I was careful to pick each lock completely from the boll. Only once do I remember looking back down my rows and noticing I had goose picked a few bolls. Instead of going back and cleaning the burs, I just prayed to God no one would notice it. Should it be discovered, however, my prayer was, "Please, God, don't let anyone tell Daddy about it," knowing full well I might receive punishment if he discovered that I was guilty of such carelessness.

By the time I was eight, I could pick about 150 pounds a day, more than most of the adults; 100 pounds was considered average for them. Each fall I increased my daily average; by the time I was 13, my average was 250-300 pounds. I was quite proud of myself. I heard there were cotton-picking contests held somewhere in Arkansas each year, and I thought, *if only I could enter one such contest, I'd be sure to win!*

When I was seven, Daddy assigned me a cow to milk daily, but I never became adept at that chore, and must have been allergic to something connected with milking; each time I went to the barnyard to milk, I returned to the house looking pale and nursing an excruciating headache. Mother became aware of my ashen looks each time and occasionally paused in her work to massage my forehead briefly.

Once, my cow lifted her right rear leg, as if deliberately, and placed that foot squarely on my left foot. It was terribly painful! Daddy was standing nearby and observed what happened, but he offered no help.

When the cow finally raised her leg, Daddy's only remark was, "I guess you'll learn not to sit up under your cow from now on." I was so young it was necessary for me to sit up under the cow to reach her teats.

We always raised hogs (swine) for family consumption and to sell for extra cash. They grow quickly and provide delicious meat – as well as a quick return of cash. I was about eight years old when Daddy came into the house one day, holding a tiny piglet.

He handed it to me and said, "Here, Ruby is the runt of a litter of fourteen pigs. The other pigs will kill it. If you will care for it and it lives, I'll give you the money when we sell it and the others."

Oh, with what tender care I nursed that pig! It grew into a fine hog, every bit as large as the largest of the others. I was so excited when Daddy returned from the sale barn late in the afternoon the day the hogs were hauled to market. He had been drinking, as always. I waited in suspense, but Daddy never offered the cash.

After supper, I timidly sidled up to him and said, "Daddy, how much money did my pig bring today?"

"Fourteen dollars," he replied.

"Where is my money?"

Daddy gave no answer; he just laughed with that drunken wet gurgling sound in his throat.

I knew better than to pursue the matter, but I shall never forget my disappointment and hurt feelings.

We raised sorghum, some of which was fed to farm animals; with the rest, we made delicious sorghum molasses for family consumption. Each year when the sorghum was ripe, I was responsible for accompanying Horton to the field to cut some stalks and toss them over the fence to the stock in the adjoining pasture. I held several stalks together to form a sheaf; then Horton cut through each one with a scythe. Once, the scythe missed the sheaf and came down on my head instead, making a sizeable wound to my head. Horton led me back to the house.

When Mother saw me and heard how the accident happened, she grabbed the can of coal oil (kerosene), which always stood on the back porch, and doused my wound with it before bandaging my head with a clean rag. I never saw a doctor but healed nicely and missed no time performing my daily chores.

When the corn fields ripened, Mother served the family fresh corn daily and canned enough to last the family until the following year. The remaining corn was allowed to dry before harvesting it to make meal, hominy, and feed for the barnyard animals.

The dried corn was harvested by wagon loads, pulled by a team of mules. The wagon always straddled a row, leaving the stalks under it broken and bent to the ground. I was always told to pull the ears of corn from the "down row," the most difficult and back-breaking job, for it required constantly bending over, pulling the corn from each stalk, then straightening up to toss it into the wagon. I could rest my back only between the time each wagon load was hauled to the barn, emptied, and returned to repeat the process until all the corn fields were harvested.

A neighbor who lived about a mile and a half down the road offered to give us his weekly newspaper when he was finished with it. Fetching the newspaper also became my weekly errand.

When the older members of the family saw I worked diligently at any job assigned, they began to disappear any time there was work to be done. I remember often hearing, "Let Ruby do it." Or, "Send Ruby."

On winter evenings, they would say, "Ruby, pop us some popcorn." Or, "Ruby, roast us some peanuts." Or, "Ruby, make us some potato chips."

I popped popcorn over hot coals pulled near the front of the fireplace. I roasted peanuts in the oven of our old wood-burning stove and deep-fried potato chips on top of it. If the chips were sliced thinly and cooked to a golden brown in Mother's freshly rendered lard, then salted properly, oh, how much superior they were in taste to the commercial ones we eat today!

In 1992, Joe and I attended B.T., an older brother, and Mary Lou's golden wedding anniversary celebration. I was reintroduced to a former Poplar Ridge neighbor with whom I had picked cotton as a child but had not seen in the 45-plus intervening years.

Following our greeting and becoming reacquainted, she asked, "Ruby, do you still work as hard as you did when you were a child?" followed by, "You always worked so hard, and I used to feel so sorry for you."

"I have never allowed much grass to grow under my feet," was my response.

SCHOOL DAYS AT POPLAR RIDGE (1939-45)

Though a Dyer County public school, the one-room Poplar Ridge Schoolhouse was located on the Obion side of the road, only about ½ mile west of our house. There were usually 20 to 25 scholars in attendance each year from the surrounding area, representing grades one through six. (Neither the school building, our farmhouse, nor the road is still in existence.)

My years at the school were from 1939-1945. Miss Maurene Corum taught first grade; Mrs. Elizabeth Crockett taught me the remaining years. She and her husband, Mr. Coulter Crockett, lived in Trimble, in a Victorian-style house scarcely a block from Trimble's main street. Its doors were always open to parents and students who were in town and dropped by for a visit.

Mrs. Crockett was of medium height and possessed a rather full, rotund body. Her long, light-brown hair was divided into about a dozen sections in the front, making as many parts. Each tress was crimped toward the back of her head, then all of them drawn together, forming a tight knot, which she pinned down securely. She was always neatly dressed, stern but compassionate, considerate, and kind.

The Crocketts never had children, but Mrs. Crockett knew how to teach and how to handle youngsters. She was in complete control and countenanced no misbehavior. She once had to discipline a hulking 16-year-old fourth grader who threatened her with a knife. She calmly, if hurriedly, dismissed all the other students for an extra recess. I was horrified, thinking the young man would surely kill her. However, in a few minutes she opened the back door and waved her handkerchief, signaling "books" again. When we entered the room, her assailant sat quietly in his seat, head down; the knife lay on the teacher's desk. She began class perfectly calm, as though she had just been presented with an apple! I have no memory of any further discipline problems during the five years I was her student.

Mrs. Crockett read the Bible daily to her students, usually from one of the Psalms or from I Corinthians 13, "When I was a child…" I did not understand the meanings of those scriptures, but I memorized many of them, for she read the same ones over and over.

By any standard of measurement, Mrs. Crockett was an outstanding teacher. Besides teaching the three "Rs," she invented games to help us remember the correct spelling of words. She held spelling bees, pitting students against their parents. She played games with us, both inside and outside. She planned programs for special occasions to which she invited the parents, and each student was expected to participate in some way. Once she chose a boy and me to sing "Reuben and Rachel," then leave the improvised stage holding hands. Oh, how it embarrassed me!

Occasionally she handed out crayons and paper and gave students time to draw freehand anything they wished. Sometimes, on cold winter days, she brought a huge pot of dried beans and cooked them on the pot-bellied stove that stood in the center of the room, near the back of the building. By lunchtime they were tender and ready to serve, and she gave each student a large serving. What a nutritious and welcomed lunch treat for the youngsters, most of whom were used to scanty meals at home.

My admiration for Mrs. Crockett knew no bounds, and her positive influence has remained with me. She brought her lunch each day, as did all the students. Each item of her food was separately wrapped to perfection. Often her lunch consisted of a few crackers filled with peanut butter, accompanied with sweet pickles. I took note of how she held her hands and curved her fingers as she ate. Then I did my best to mimic her manners at home if we ever had peanut butter and crackers to eat, along with Mother's homemade sweet pickles.

Looking back, I think Mrs. Crockett must have felt a special tenderness for me. No doubt, she knew of my difficult home life and that I was an apt and conscientious student. I walked the half mile to school each day and was always the first student to arrive. In the winter, my hands were cold and swollen, for I owned neither gloves nor cap. Mrs. Crockett would already have a fire blazing in the big pot-bellied stove when I arrived. She would station a chair near it, lift me to her lap, and place my little frozen fingers in her hair and distract me with some pretty tale until my hands were warm. Sometimes she told me secrets and said I must keep them "under my hat." I didn't know exactly what that meant – nor did I own a hat. Still, I never disclosed anything she told me at such times. And I understood I must jump down from her lap when we heard footsteps on the front porch, signaling other students' arrival.

I was in fourth grade the time I asked permission to go to the bathroom, an outhouse several yards down the steepest side of the hill on which the schoolhouse stood. A split log formed a bridge over the last few feet of the downward-sloping path leading to the outhouse. It was a rainy day, and the log was slick. I hurried along, and just as I jumped onto the log, my feet slipped; I fell off, breaking my left arm rather badly. I ran back up the hill, crying and in shock.

As soon as I could manage, between sobs, to inform Mrs. Crockett what had happened, she suspended class and again took me onto her ample lap, this time openly before the other students. She promptly sent someone for Mother and held me, comforted and consoled me when I repeatedly asked her, "Will I die? Will I die?"

Someone in the community who owned a car drove Mother and me to Dyersburg to a doctor who set the fractured bones and placed my arm in a cast. Some six weeks later, that Good Samaritan took me back to the doctor to have the cast removed, revealing a shriveled left arm much smaller than the right one, leading me to think I would always be "deformed." However, it wasn't long until it had regained its normal proportions.

The Christmas following my 10th birthday, I received a special surprise at school. It came at the end of our Christmas program, when I had finished reciting "'Twas the Night before Christmas" by Clement C. Moore and returned to my seat. Mother sat beside me, for she attended special events at school whenever possible.

Then it was time to distribute the gifts piled under the Christmas tree, and Mrs. Crockett performed that task, handing the last package to me. When I unwrapped and opened the box, inside was a doll wearing a lovely spring dress over snow-white underclothes. On her head was a spring straw hat, beneath which fell beautiful blonde tresses. Coordinating shoes and socks completed her ensemble. How her blue eyes sparkled! I thought her the most beautiful doll in the whole world and was so completely overcome with joy, I could not restrain the tears that streamed down my cheeks, for she was the first (and only) doll I ever owned as a child. How I cared for her! I thought her much too pretty for play, but there was no place in our house to exhibit her, so I kept her in her box and hid her in secret hiding places. I didn't want anyone to find her or handle her and perhaps soil her garments.

When I married years later, that doll came along, wherever my husband and I happened to live. Her skin eventually cracked all over, so I reluctantly discarded her. At that time, I was not aware that I might have sought a professional to have her restored. However, I shall never forget the joy of owning that doll and the sacrifice Mother must have made to purchase such a fine gift for me.

TRIMBLE SCHOOL
YEARS (1945-47)

Rural Poplar Ridge School served only the first six grades. Continued formal education required students to attend Trimble School for their high-school years. School buses ran routes to collect and bring the pupils in the morning and return them home at the close of the school day. The bus I caught every day ran a second route, so I had to be ready to leave home at 6 a.m., to allow sufficient time to deliver the first group of students at 7 and end the second route no later than 8, when the bell signaled the start of class.

All students arriving early had to sit in the library during the intervening hour and study or remain quiet while others studied. A resident of the town was employed to monitor study hall for that time period each day. To ask for help with class work or for permission to go to the bathroom, a student must first raise his hand to be recognized, after which he/she must stand and politely ask, "May I...?"

Once when a girl raised her hand and was recognized, she rose from her seat, and with stammering, stuttering difficulty, asked, "May I see an en-, en-, encycropedia?"

Permission granted!

It was at Trimble School I was first introduced to basketball, and it was an instant love affair, and basketball remains my favorite sport today. I became a guard and was given an ensemble of gear to wear for games. Often one of my classmates who lived beside the railroad tracks in town invited me to spend the night with her during evening games, so I could dress out in my prized uniform and high-top tennis shoes. How thrilling! However, I always awakened with a start when the night train/s passed through with their whistles blowing full blast; it took me some seconds to remember it was not some destructive explosion I was hearing but a train passing through on its way to Memphis or to Chicago.

One evening a young man asked permission to take me home after a game. He was in high school and I only in eighth grade. Another couple went along, and the young men took us to a tiny café in Trimble for sandwiches and sodas. It was the first time I had ever eaten out or had been on any semblance of a date. I was embarrassed and had no idea what to order. Timidly I finally managed to ask for a bacon, lettuce, and tomato sandwich and a Pepsi Cola. My escort drove me home afterward. I have no recollection whether he walked me to the door, but I suppose he did. I do well remember he was kind and mannerly toward me.

I have only a few outstanding memories of my two years at Trimble School. I studied the usual required subjects and grew quite fond of studying English; I particularly enjoyed diagramming sentences. In eighth grade I was permitted to study home economics as an elective; the study of those two subjects became my lifelong love.

My seventh-grade science teacher was the minister for one of the local churches. The students called him "Brother D." I vividly recall the day we were assigned a chapter with a monkey's picture on one of the pages. When we turned to that page, as we read the chapter aloud in class, Brother D asked me what I thought of the monkey's picture.

After studying the picture a few seconds, with sincere childish honesty, I replied, "It looks just like Sam ____ to me!" He was a member of my class.

Brother D. quickly continued with the class without further comment. I have thought about that incident many times in my adulthood and wondered if I were "proving evolution," though at the time I had never heard of the word and hadn't the least idea what it meant! Nor did it occur to me at the time that I might have been insulting my classmate.

My grade average for the two years of junior-high school was 98+ percent, and I graduated as salutatorian of the class. My classmate who was the valedictorian, managed only a small fraction of one percent grade higher than mine. All the girls wore white dresses for the graduation ceremony. For the occasion, Mother ordered me a white cotton eyelet dress with a peplum. The one outstanding memory I have about the graduation program is that the high-school chorus sang the hymn "Out of the Ivory Palaces," a song I had never heard before, and it struck a spiritual chord in me. It remains one of my favorite hymns.

HARDSHIPS AND PAIN

My sister Virginia was called "Fudge," a nickname she earned as a child because she always fudged (cheated) at the game of marbles. She married Lloyd Devasier in September 1934 and both moved into our house to live. She gave birth to twin sons, Ralph Jerry and Ray Terry, on November 1, 1935, just weeks before I turned two. Virginia chose to make her home with our family after her children were born. Lloyd eventually left the area and joined the U.S. Coast Guard sometime during the late 1930s. He was killed soon after our country entered WWII and lies buried in the American Cemetery in the Philippines. His tombstone states the death as February 26, 1942. Virginia, Ralph, and Ray remained a permanent part of our household for more than 10 years.

Ralph and Ray were fine-looking children and received a great deal of attention, but little discipline. Daddy showed open partiality toward them. My brother B.T. (named after Daddy, who was named for the minister, Ballie Taylor, who agreed to officiate at his parents' wedding ceremony for nothing if they promised to name their first son after him) was always my friend and protector. He cursed Daddy one day when he heard Daddy say he loved Ralph and Ray but not Ruby. Daddy offered the excuse that Ralph and Ray had no father to love them.

B.T. replied, "Neither does Ruby have a father if you don't love her."

The twins were quite mischievous and spoiled. Acting in concert, they soon exercised complete control over me. One day I made a playhouse in the backyard, using the only playthings I ever had: a few broken pieces of dishes, discarded bottles, empty cans, scraps of wood, etc. Ray came along just when I had finished arranging all the "furniture" and kicked everything apart, then ran across the yard as fast as his little legs could carry him. I gave chase and administered a solid smack across his shoulder when I caught up with him. Ralph was standing nearby, holding an old rusty hatchet in his hand. Seeing I had hit Ray, he ran after me, hatchet in hand, and struck me on the head with it, summoning all the force of his young body. Fortunately, the blade was quite dull, or he might have made an end of me. However, it was sharp enough to leave a sizeable wound on my head. Mother cleaned the site and again applied some coal oil to stop the bleeding. She kept my head bound with clean white rags until the wound healed. Ralph and Ray went unpunished. Both Daddy and Virginia dismissed the incident, calmly remarking, "Ruby had no business hitting Ray!" - their exact words.

As a child I was plagued for many years with a painful condition, tiny pin worms lodged in my lower colon area. When the pain became so intense that I made Mother aware of it, she would give me a warm soapy enema to expel the worms and relieve me. Once, when there was no other bed space available, I had to sleep between Daddy and Mother. I understood it was taboo to awaken Daddy, but during the night I began to hurt so badly I could not help sobbing – as quietly as possible.

When my crying awakened Daddy, he said not a word but slapped me across the face with a strong hand. Awakened, Mother arose and proceeded to give me an enema, which relieved me greatly. I do not know what medication she eventually discovered to rid me of that agonizing and embarrassing condition, but I have never since been so afflicted.

Another time when a near neighbor sat in our front room, visiting with Daddy, I was in the room and asked our guest some question, but forgot to address him with the title of "Mister." For that infraction of the rules, Daddy stepped over and struck me so hard I was momentarily dazed. When I revived, the visitor was correcting Daddy for such severe punishment. I was so wholly overcome with humiliation and pain, I made a quick exit from the room.

There was another relative who held little affection for me. It would embarrass my readers and me if I related some of the most hurtful and painful ways she humiliated me; hence, I will relate only a couple of the lesser incidents. She told me one day that my stomach protruded so much I looked pregnant. I did not know what that descriptive word meant, but I understood it was no compliment, and I cried. Another time she told me my shoulders were crooked and I was so stooped I would never have any friends. Again, I cried, but kept my hurt feelings to myself. If Mother ever learned about any mistreatment of me, as she sometimes did, she would reprimand the offending one with these words: "The child should not be treated that way."

When I was growing up, children were required to wait for the adults to finish eating before they had a turn at the table. It was often that I must wait for the "second" or "third table" in our large family, especially on Sundays when both neighbors and relatives who lived nearby set their feet under Mother's table.

I recall the only time Mother made me a birthday cake when I was still a child. How excited I felt and could hardly wait for my turn at the second table. Mother placed the cake on the table when the "grown folks" were eating, but she told them it was my birthday and some of the cake must be left for me and the other children to enjoy. She was unaware that they gobbled up every bite of the cake as soon as Mother turned her back. When I came to the table and saw the empty cake plate, I cried. Mother was sorry also, but what could be said to a group of adults who would treat a child in that way, even laugh heartily about their "trick"?

Children have no choice but to accept the environment in which they are reared. Later in life they may analyze their upbringing. Though I hold no animosity toward any of my relatives, in some childish way I realized Daddy and others of the family held no love for me. It should not be surprising that early in life I became a fearful child, and that feeling persisted. I obeyed Daddy and older siblings, but their attitude toward and treatment of me resulted in my being a shy, timid child, feeling inferior to others. I tried to mask my intimidation, but I struggled for many years with such feelings, far into adulthood.

Mother was my inspiration, however, to work hard, get an education, strive to overcome poverty and rise above all difficult circumstances and "be somebody" (her exact words). I have tried diligently to follow her teaching, and God has answered all my sincere prayers, and the blessings have been many in the latter years. Albeit belatedly, I finally overcame my inferiority complex. I credit Mother and the few who encouraged me along the way for anything I have ever achieved.

LESSONS LEARNED "OUT OF SCHOOL"

Mother was always protective of all nature. One of her rules specified that a bird's nest containing eggs or baby birds should never be disturbed; else the mother bird would abandon the nest. Once, when returning from the garden where Mother had sent me to fetch some onions, I spotted a bird's nest on a low tree branch near the garden gate. It was within my reach; and though I remembered Mother's admonition, I could not resist the urge that came over me. Ever so gently, I placed my small hand in the nest.

Mother could always "read" me. When I returned to the kitchen, she quickly took note of the guilty look on my face, for she said, "Ruby Clone, what have you been doing?"

I confessed my misdemeanor, telling Mother exactly what I had done; and I received Mother's usual means of punishment, a spanking.

On another occasion, a neighbor who owned a truck was driving a sick person from our community to Trimble to see Dr. Wright. Several neighboring children and I (the youngest) were allowed to go along, riding in the back of the truck. Dr. Wright had a sizeable orchard at the back of his house, which adjoined his tiny office. The fence surrounding the orchard was three feet high or more. We youngsters were left in the truck while the patient was being seen. We looked around and spotted the good doctor's orchard filled with peach trees loaded with beautiful peaches at the peak of their ripeness. One of the older boys, Tim ___, quickly climbed the fence and helped himself to several of the glorious orbs. When he returned with his loot, he and the others began to dare me to go for more peaches. I knew I shouldn't do so, but the dares continued, and I yielded to my fondness for peaches, a delicacy we rarely had at home. With difficulty, I climbed over the fence and helped myself to two peaches.

I never knew how Mother discovered my theft, but she reprimanded me severely. In addition, the next trip into town, she placed a nickel in my hand, took me to Dr. Wright's office and left me with instructions to apologize to the doctor and hand him the nickel as payment for the peaches. There I sat in the patients' waiting room, alone, frightened, embarrassed and fearful. By the time Dr. Wright called for me, his next "patient," I meekly entered his office, overcome with tears. I managed somehow to heed Mother's instructions to apologize and hand him the nickel.

Dr. Wright knew our family, for he had often sent for Mother to assist him on newborn calls in our community. He knew of my home life, too – Daddy's reputation was known far and wide in West Tennessee.

When I had finished my errand, Dr. Wright placed the nickel back in my hand and put his arm around me and spoke these kind words, "Ruby, I want you to buy yourself an ice-cream cone with this nickel before you go home, but don't ever get into my peach orchard again without my permission."

Lessons learned permanently!

RECREATION AND SOCIAL LIFE

There was no such thing as vacations in our family when I was growing up. There was no means of travel for the Yateses other than walking, riding in a wagon pulled by mules, or riding horseback. We didn't own a radio until sometime during WWII, and B.T. purchased a truck some time during that period. It was used for our family, as well as to accommodate neighbors' errands. However, even the poorest people can enjoy and share simple pleasures. To the extent of her ability and means, Mother wanted her children to be cultivated, hospitable, and sociable. She shared anything and everything with those around her, usually at the cost of depriving herself.

Mother permitted the older brothers and sisters to invite neighbors and friends over to play cards and games whenever possible. One young gentleman, J.T. McCollum, often brought his guitar to play and sing for the group. My older siblings always closed the door to the better of our two front rooms at these parties, and my feelings were always hurt because I was never permitted to enter and share in their gaieties or refreshments.

When the crops were laid by, the family occasionally enjoyed a summer outing on the banks of the Obion River, a fork of which flowed through the woods a short distance past our fields. Once, we spent the night there. Over an open fire, Mother fried fish and potatoes and cooked whatever other vegetables were in season at the time. All except Mother and me, played and swam in the river. I did not know how to swim; but one time,

B.T. swam to the bank of the river where I was standing and told me to climb onto his back and hold on. What a thrill I felt when he swam across the river and back with me! I can still feel the joy of that day's experience.

Our cows produced more milk daily than our family needed, so Mother usually had butter, cream, and milk to sell when the milk truck came by every other day. There was also plenty of milk, rich cream, and eggs for making ice cream. Ice from the ice house in Trimble was delivered to our rural area twice weekly. Mother ordered a specific amount of ice each delivery and kept it in the big ice box, which stood on our back porch. She kept it covered with old woolen blankets; with thrifty use, the ice would last from one delivery to the next. Sometimes during summer months Mother ordered extra ice for making ice cream. Nearby neighbors were always invited, making it a social occasion. Three or four gallons was the standard amount required each time.

After Mother prepared all the ice cream mixes, they were emptied into the canisters and placed inside the hand-cranked wooden ice-cream freezers and placed on the back porch. These were then packed with crushed ice and salt and covered with papers, old blankets, or whatever was available. The younger children sat atop the freezers while the men constantly turned the handles of the cranks until the mix was soft frozen. The dasher was then pulled from the center of the canister and licked clean by whoever was lucky enough to get it. Then the freezers were salted and packed with ice a final time. Covered once again, they were allowed to rest for a few minutes, to ensure the ice cream was firm throughout. Afterward, all were served until sated, while sitting around on the back porch, or on the porch steps, laughing and talking, as we relished that delicious "food of the gods."

B.T. kept a record of the week's total amount of cotton picked by each hand. At the end of each week, Daddy paid the amount owed to every worker, except his family members. He sometimes permitted us to lay aside our cotton sacks early on Saturdays, especially if we had a load of cotton ready for him to haul to the gin and collect money for it. On those occasions, Daddy would give us each a quarter or a half dollar, so we could go to see a picture show on Saturday night at Newbern, a few miles south of Trimble. The movie cost 11 cents, so we had enough money left for popcorn or snack crackers and a Coke, or even a hamburger if we had received a 50-cent piece. Our transportation was communal, and several of us rode in the back of the truck with whichever neighbor provided it.

A western movie was always shown on Saturdays, and it provided the topic of conversation in the cotton fields the entire following week. The young boys in particular delighted in discussing the good guys versus the bad guys over and over, reaching various conclusions of their own!

Daddy did not show up in the field except when the cotton wagon was loaded and ready for our mules to be attached and pull the wagon to the gin, for there he collected the money for the ginned cotton bale produced by each load. Only once did Daddy allow me to remove my sack and ride with him the three miles to the cotton gin in Trimble. I clearly recall what a mild and perfect fall day it was. For the entire trip to town, I lay atop the soft cotton and looked up at the "porch of heaven," a sky filled with fluffy, snow-white clouds, and I tried to make as many figures of them as my mind could imagine. Perhaps it was the beauty of that flawless day that subconsciously softened Daddy's heart enough for him to permit me to make that trip with him, but I'm sure he never once thought about what a beautiful – even inspiring, and permanent – picture it brought to my mind.

Some neighbors who moved from our community returned on visits to our family. I recall two such families who asked permission for me to go home with them for a few days. Mother granted permission. I was treated with love, which made me feel really special. The friends would let me participate in their work, far lighter than what I was used to performing at home, so it always seemed like child's play for me.

Once, however, my weekend visit with two friends, a brother and sister, ended in embarrassment. I had brought one change of clothes in a brown paper bag. As we three walked down the lane from their house to meet the school bus on Monday morning, I dropped my bag; out fell the pair of soiled undies I had placed in the top of the bag. I hurriedly retrieved them and stuffed them back into the bag. Both of my friends were aware of my embarrassment, but they merely laughed heartily and said nothing. I never heard that they told anyone about the incident, for I prayed they wouldn't! God does hear and answer children's prayers!

One Sunday morning Mr. Morris, flew to his farm in his small two-seater airplane and landed on his landing strip near our house. He came to our house to ask whether I would like to take a ride in his airplane.

"Yes, Sir!" I replied.

After securing the necessary permission from Mother, away we went! He flew over all his land and called my attention to our house as he dipped low to fly directly overhead. In my older years, I never enjoy flying and sometimes grow anxious during flights, especially when there is turbulence; but for that flight I was far too excited to be frightened.

Though we rarely had opportunity to see our relatives from either side of the family, Mother wanted her children to get to know her people. Those who had the means visited us some, but we rarely saw Daddy's relatives; his lifestyle did not encourage their coming. The lone exception was Daddy's sister, Aunt Savannah Jones, who lived with us for long periods of time after she was widowed.

A few times Mother saved money sufficient to buy a round-trip bus ticket for me to visit her youngest sister, my Aunt Lona Roberts, and her family, who lived within the city limits of Fulton, Kentucky. Riding the Greyhound bus from Trimble to Fulton, approximately 35 miles from my narrow world, was a huge event for me, and I was certain I was traveling across the entire country!

Aunt Lona and Uncle Shelby were always kind to me. Uncle Shelby was a railroad employee, whose work required him to work nights and sleep in the daytime. Aunt Lona used to whisper in my ear that I must speak very quietly when Uncle Shelby was sleeping. I tried to obey but was so used to speaking loudly into Mother's ears, sometimes I forgot; nor did I understand at the time why anyone slept all day long!

Though I was still a preteen, Aunt Lona always insisted her two teenage children, Frances and Glen, take me along anywhere they went. I do not recall that they ever complained – certainly not in my presence – but they probably resented having to take an ignorant little country cousin along with them to visit their friends in the city.

DADDY'S DEATH
AND AFTERMATH

In February 1946, much of our cotton still stood in the field, owing to an unusually wet fall. Having stood for months exposed to the inhospitable weather, the locks of cotton were dingy and dirty, their upper portions drooping and sagging helplessly while their lower ones were captured tightly in the shrunken burs, now sharp as rose briars. The cotton's quality was greatly diminished; in this condition, it could not be picked. The entire bolls must be pulled.

On Monday morning, February 26, 1946 Daddy instructed Horton and me as we left for school, "Beginning tomorrow, you must stay home until the cotton is pulled, so tell your teachers you will not be in school again for a while."

With regret, I dutifully obeyed Daddy.

Before daybreak the next morning, Mother lay awake already when Daddy returned to bed after arising momentarily to call Horton to build a fire in the Warm Morning coal stove, which stood a few feet in front of the fireplace, then in disuse. Instead of lying down again in his accustomed way, Daddy fell to the bed with such a thud Mother felt the entire bed shake. She heard a gurgling noise issue from Daddy's throat.

Alarmed, she turned toward him to ask, "What is the matter with you, Mr. Yates?" (Mother always called Daddy, "Mr. Yates," and he called her "Wife.")

No response came, for the swiftness of death had already sealed his lips forever.

An autopsy revealed Daddy had experienced a massive heart attack. It further revealed his heart had been damaged by an earlier one. Then Mother recalled how a few months earlier Daddy had returned from the barnyard late one afternoon with excruciating chest pains. She quickly prepared a glass of soda water for him, thinking it was perhaps a case of indigestion. Daddy drank it and lay across the bed until the pain subsided. He never saw a doctor; nor had there been any further warning.

After embalming, Daddy's body was returned to the house, where the family and neighbors sat watch both day and night, as was the custom then, until it was buried four days later, allowing time for his eldest son, Webb, to arrive with his family from a distant city. My science instructor, Brother D. officiated at Daddy's funeral, though Daddy was not a member of his congregation – nor any other.

Mother made arrangements for Daddy to be buried beside his first wife, Beulah (Lowrance) Yates, for she was sure that would have been his choice. They lie in Salem Cemetery in Gibson County, Tennessee, interred along the same row of graves as many of Daddy's Yates ancestors.

Daddy's family had been penniless for many years; nor was there any insurance or other means of paying the funeral expenses. Some of the married children pooled money to cover the costs. Still, no tombstone marked Daddy and Beulah's graves until 1996 when I purchased one, 50 years after Daddy's death and 80 after Beulah's. Joe insisted I give notice of my plans, so I wrote each sibling a letter – but asked for no assistance. I received a response and a small donation from only three of them.

Horton was 15 when Daddy died, and I'd turned 12 the previous November. We were the only children still living at home. Both of us were seasoned farm workers, having been put to the plow at an early age; still, neither we nor Mother was capable of farming independently as sharecroppers. It was our older brother B.T. who had always helped Daddy with the farm work and who accepted more and more responsibility for both families as Daddy's drinking habits rendered him less and less capable.

After B.T. married and started his own family, he remained on the Morris farm and worked in partnership with Daddy; that is, he assumed both his and Daddy's responsibility to farm 100 acres, with the help other family members could provide.

The year following Daddy's decease, Mother continued the farming partnership with B.T. for one crop, but a large portion of the responsibilities fell to him. Mother realized she could no longer continue in her present circumstances. She assured B.T. she had no intention of leaning on him for her livelihood. What was she to do? She was 46 years old, had no formal education above fourth grade, and her entire life's experiences had revolved around household duties. Never had she held a public job.

Painfully aware of her limitations, Mother decided to leave the farm in the spring of 1947. She secured a job at Salant & Salant, Inc., one of the two factories in Obion. Both factories employed women almost exclusively to cut and sew men's shirts. Mother worked on a production line for the next 13 years or so. I lacked six weeks finishing eighth grade, so I remained behind with B.T. and Mary Lou until my school year ended.

THE OBION YEARS (1947-51)

Virginia had been estranged from Lloyd for several years before he was killed in the War, but she had never divorced him, so she was able to file for a widow's pension for herself and the twins. She drew Lloyd's insurance and assistance for the boys until they were grown. She saved every penny of the income until she had a sufficient amount to purchase a modest house in Obion, where she moved just prior to Daddy's death and Mother's consequent move there. The three of us – Mother, Horton, and I – lived temporarily in two rooms on one side of Virginia's house and shared a bath.

Horton convinced Mother to sign a document which allowed him to join the military just as soon as he turned 16, leaving the two of us alone. He injured his back severely after serving only a few years and was honorably discharged and eventually provided with a military pension.

As soon as possible, Mother purchased an old, weather-worn four-room frame house, which soon burned down. A builder by trade, one of my brothers-in-law, Wallace Martin, assisted by some of my brothers, built Mother a new one on the lot; for she had no insurance or other means to replace her loss.

WORK ADDICT

Though I had not reached my 14th birthday, I had been grown since I was 11. More than one neighbor guessed I was 16 or 17 when I was only 11 and already wore a size-nine ladies' shoe!

Those who know me well will tell anyone I am a workaholic – which undoubtedly springs from those impressionable young years when responsibilities consumed almost all of my waking hours. I am now well into my ninth decade, and I continue to work, but at a slower pace. It is just recently my daughters have stopped saying, "Mother, you can work circles around us any time!"

In our new location, it never occurred to me to be dependent on Mother for my support. She paid all household expenses, but I earned sufficient money to pay all my personal and school expenses. Within a few days after my move to Obion, I had a full-time summer job as waitress for the small café, Little Victory. It was situated at a desirable location on U.S. Highway 51. It served fresh hot meals daily, except on Sunday, at reasonable prices. Local customers flocked there regularly; also, being on a major north-south highway, travelers often stopped there.

Breakfast was cooked on the grill. A fresh, varied lunch menu was prepared daily and consisted of meat, vegetables, bread, and delicious pies. Lunch always lasted until everything cooked for that day had been served. Thereafter, sandwiches and light foods were served until closing time at 9 – except during basketball season, when the cafe remained open an hour or so after the high school's basketball home games, mainly to accommodate young people and others who liked to gather and rehash the games over a snack and a cup of coffee or a Coke, while the nickelodeon blared out the popular songs of the day.

I first worked from 10 a.m.-6 p.m., but after a few weeks, the owner asked me to work the early shift, 6 a.m.-2 p.m. In doing so, I served breakfast to customers, which I prepared by myself for the first three hours when the owner arrived to begin preparing the noon meals. Looking back, I'm not sure how I managed it, but I must have done satisfactory work, for I worked my first two summers there and met many local people in that way. During the four years I was an Obion resident, I became acquainted with all her citizens and others from the outlying areas if they did their shopping there. Some became loyal friends whose encouragement played a role in my future plans.

Beer was served at the cafe, but as I was underage, I was forbidden to serve it; I gladly complied. Once, two men just traveling through ordered beers, and I asked another employee to serve it, as I always did. However, the men kept eyeing me and made some kind of improper remark to me, likely thinking I was much older. I probably did not even know what the remark had meant, so naïve was I at the time. Fortunately, the owner heard them and swiftly came to my rescue by ordering them to leave. They did so, and there was never another such incident. Thank God for that earthly angel!

* * *

While working at Little Victory the first summer, I met the owner's nephew, Bobby Rutherford, who lived with her. He was a few years my senior and a fine young Christian man. Soon, Bobby asked if I were willing to visit the minister of the Church of Christ for some Bible lessons. I agreed, and for several weeks he occasionally came by the café at the end of my workday and walked with me to Minister Stovall's house, where he proceeded to teach me Bible lessons.

When I decided to visit the worship services, an acquaintance attempted to dissuade me, saying those people were very "peculiar," along with some other uncomplimentary remarks. The more she said, the greater became my curiosity, so I determined to visit there to observe firsthand and form my own opinion of these Christians rumored to be so very odd.

Mother had prepared me to accept the simple truths of the Bible, so after visiting the congregation, I never attended services at either of Obion's other two churches, though I had been kindly received when I had visited them earlier. Soon I was converted. Though often falling short, I have continued to try to learn and to grow in Christ's kingdom and shall always remember my friend Bobby for his assistance.

I was eager to learn everything possible, still am, and always full of questions. Though all the women in the church wore hats at the time, a question in vogue among them was whether Scripture required it. I wanted to know the correct answer to that question and persisted in asking every minister I met. Each offered a different response. Confused, I finally decided I must find the answer for myself. I read and reread the first part of I Corinthians 11 and concluded the safe thing to do was to wear a hat as a second covering over the hair, the first covering. As soon as I could afford to purchase one, I began wearing a hat and have never stopped, though I never forced my conviction on anyone else. I have been criticized a few times for doing so after the practice was discontinued.

Another time, I innocently asked an embarrassing question of the man who taught the Sunday-morning teenage class. We were studying sins of the flesh. When we came to lasciviousness, I asked the brother to please define that word. Perhaps I embarrassed him, or maybe he did not know how best to explain its meaning to me, for he stammered and stuttered a few minutes, leaving me totally confused! When I later came to understand the meaning of the word, I also felt embarrassed and surely understood and sympathized with the teacher's problem.

* * *

That fall, I entered Obion School for my freshman year. I was soon working every Saturday as a clerk in Turney's Grocery store, owned by Rex and LaGreta Turney. In addition, I worked a few hours alternate Fridays after school, when the factory employees were paid and came by to settle their previous two weeks' grocery bill. This work lasted my entire four years of high school.

Soon I became acquainted with Obion's only Jewish family, the Lehmans, who owned a clothing store a few doors from Turney's Grocery.

Semi-yearly they advertised a half-price sale on all the previous season's clothes remaining in stock. Each time before the sale began, one of the Lehmans would come to the grocery store and tell me to come look over their clothing and select the items I wished to purchase. After I made my selections, my name was placed inside each garment. Following their sale, they notified me of every yet-unsold item bearing my name and held them all in layaway until I paid for them at a few dollars each week. These clothes and the others I fashioned for myself became my high-school wardrobe.

Once, when Mother had to work at the factory on Saturday, her work day began at 7 a.m. She left me sleeping, and I was still asleep when Rex Turney knocked at the front door shortly after 8 a.m., when I should have been at work already.

I recognized his voice when he called my name. I jumped out of bed and admitted I was still asleep, without opening the door.

Rex waited patiently on the porch for me to get dressed and ride to work with him.

I apologized, but he never criticized or rebuked me in any way. I was embarrassed and made a special effort never to be late for work again during the four years I worked for him.

Another incident occurred while I was a Turney's Grocery employee. It was in connection with one of Obion's prominent citizens, a friend and customer of Turney's Grocery. During that time, recyclable glass milk bottles were in use, and a two-cent deposit was charged on all bottles purchased, unless the customer brought along empty bottles in exchange. Sometimes customers forgot to bring their empty bottles along and were forgiven – until the practice was much abused.

One day, La Greta instructed me, "Ruby, from now on, any time customers fail to bring in empty bottles for exchange when they purchase milk, you will have to charge the two-cents deposit – without exception."

Who would be one of my next customers but the afore-mentioned gentleman? He was one of the customers who almost never returned empty bottles. As was his custom, he went straight to the cooler where the milk was kept, made his usual selection of two quarts of sweet milk and brought them to the counter, where I was the only clerk working the counter at that moment.

Though I saw him when he came in and knew already he had come "empty handed," I kindly asked him, "Sir, did you bring your empty bottles today?"

"No!" came his curt reply, as though the mention of it was an insult to His Highness.

"Then, I'll have to charge you two cents' deposit on each bottle, today and in the future if you forget to bring empty bottles to exchange for your milk purchase," thinking I had properly obeyed my boss's instruction with no thought of offense.

However, with an intimidating frown, the man snatched the two bottles of milk from the counter, returned them to the cooler, and hastily exited the store with no further word to me.

Soon afterward the telephone rang. When La Greta answered, a voice proceeded to inform her I had spoken curtly to him when I "demanded" a bottle deposit from him. I heard her on the phone for what seemed at least 15 minutes. She seemed to be struggling for words, and I thought something must be amiss, but it never occurred to me the problem had to do with me.

When she was finally able to conclude the conversation, La Greta came to me, looking quite harassed. "Ruby, I know you were doing exactly what I told you to do, and you did the right thing. I also know that you are never curt with any customer, but in the future, don't ever dare mention a milk bottle deposit to Mr. ___ again!"

Another lesson learned the hard way! I never again mentioned a milk bottle deposit to that customer, though he often failed to bring bottles for the exchange. However, my sense of fairness told me something wasn't quite right to charge others and except the man who had a great deal more means than most of Obion's other citizens.

* * *

During one of my Obion years I worked the entire summer for Bertha Fox, an unmarried local native who was a retired dietitian from one of Memphis' prestigious hotels. She then returned to live among relatives and her roots and opened a fine restaurant, also on U.S. Highway 51, a distance south of the Little Victory Café where I had worked the two previous summers.

Word soon circulated about the owner's outstanding cooking skills, and people began to come from far and near to savor her meals. And Bertha was especially good and kind to me. If a friend came by during evening hours when we weren't quite busy, she often volunteered, "Ruby, why don't you leave now and enjoy being with your friend a while?" In fact, she usually insisted on my going.

During the time I worked for Bertha, I met a couple who were vacationing in our area; they ate lunch at Bertha's restaurant every day during their stay. As their waitress I became acquainted with them. One day, they invited me to spend the day with them at Reelfoot Lake on my next day off.

I accepted their kind invitation and enjoyed a delightful day fishing on the world-famous lake with them and being taken out for a tasty lunch. I never saw them again and cannot now recall their names; but my association with them, albeit brief, remains a pleasant memory.

One particularly embarrassing incident occurred that summer. One of my cousins came in one day for lunch, after which he asked whether he could pay by check. I asked Bertha, declaring our relationship, and assured her it was safe to take his check. How humiliated I was to learn from her later the check had bounced! I offered to pay her, but she steadfastly refused to allow me to do so. Another lesson learned the hard way.

* * *

The summer I graduated from high school, I tutored young Tommy Morris, son of one of Obion's prominent families, the entire summer; Tommy's teachers had told his parents Tommy must repeat fourth grade unless he could make progress with a tutor that summer.

Each weekday morning Tommy arrived on his bicycle promptly at 8 a.m. After a two-hour study session, we took a brief recess. Tommy would ride his bicycle up and down our street while I attended something inside the house. Afterward, we had another long session of study from his books. Tommy was not an eager student but an obedient one, always cooperating with me in class work and came each day with his assigned homework completed. He must have made good progress, for his parents came to me years later and said Tommy never experienced further difficulty making passing grades thereafter.

Still, years later, I was more than delighted to learn Tommy Morris had been elected as the Obion County Superintendent of Education! I still take satisfaction in the fact I had some part in teaching him the importance of diligence in study, which led to his future success.

For my tutoring, I earned $1 an hour – the highest hourly wage I had ever received to date. What a providential blessing, for I had arranged to attend business school at Memphis School of Commerce (MSC) at the end of the summer, so all my earnings were set aside for my further education.

Many other kinds of work formed parts of my high-school work repertoire: I worked in the lunch room an hour each day to earn my lunch. My classes were arranged so I had a free period to help serve the grammar-school students prior to the high-school lunch period.

Because Mother's work day at the shirt factory began at 7, she was always at work before I left for school, so I rarely ate breakfast. As a result, I was always famished by lunchtime. I shall never forget how good the hot, buttered cornbread tasted when one of the lunch-room employees offered me a slice as soon as I entered the kitchen. I would devour it quickly and be ready to help serve the youngsters as they came bounding into the lunch room.

Occasionally a grammar-school teacher would have to leave her class for a few hours. At those times, the principal would ask me to substitute teach. He always found some way to assist me in school for the work because he could not officially pay me cash as a student substitute teacher. The experience provided valuable on-the-job training, since I later taught school for a total of 17 years in Alabama, at both the secondary and the post-secondary level. In addition, I tutored privately for far more than 17 years.

I cleaned houses occasionally for affluent families in Obion and baby sat their children. For both these random jobs, I received 50 cents an hour, slightly more than I averaged per hour at Turney's Grocery, for there I worked such long hours. However, the Turneys raised my salary from $3 per Saturday to $4 during my junior and senior years; in addition, they paid me extra for my Friday afternoon work.

In my adulthood, I have performed both menial and professional work, but no employer has ever treated me with more kindness and respect than those for whom I worked during my high-school years.

OBION SCHOOL
DAYS (1947-51)

My high-school days in Obion were prior to the time of consolidated county schools. Each community had its own school, which was very much a part of the community. Obion School and its outbuildings covered several acres. The complex was comprised of the grammar school, high school, gymnasium, home-economics house, and canning facility, along with large, separate playgrounds for the grammar school and the high school.

Having the opportunity to attend school seemed always such a privilege to me; when I entered Obion School in the fall of 1947, I entered with excitement and expectancy.

At that time standard requirements for freshmen were English, math, health/science, history, and physical education. My electives included typing and home economics. I especially enjoyed studying English and home economics, and I could hardly wait for basketball season to begin.

I practiced basketball with all the strength my body could muster. Though I was only a freshman, the coach started me as a guard on the varsity team each game. How disappointing and painful – both mentally and physically – when I seriously injured my right knee in a game during my first season. At that time there was no help provided for injured players, so my injury went untreated. My leg swelled until it became almost as large around as my waist. I suffered excruciating pain for months and could walk only with the support of crutches. The principal rearranged my classes so they all met on the first floor, as I was unable to scale the long flight of stairs for many months.

Sometime later that year, the county school nurse came by our school; the principal sent me to her for a look. Upon examination, she insisted I should see a doctor, by all means. Neither Mother nor I had money or medical insurance, so I was unable to take the nurse's advice.

Though left with residual pain, by the next school year I had discarded my crutches and was excited to begin basketball practice once more. However, my fledgling career quickly ended; after just a few practices, my injured knee gave way again, and I fell, renewing the severe swelling and pain I had first experienced. Only God knows the disappointment I felt! My only consolation was being elected cheerleader for my remaining three years of high school. Cheering was much simpler then than now, so I managed to remain with my team, except when a conflict arose with my work schedule. My choice had to be work, for my employers expected as much; plus, I the fact that I needed the money.

All my teachers were good ones, and I liked and respected them. Perhaps I'm biased because my favorite teachers were those who taught my favorite subjects, home economics and English. Miss Amanda DeWeese was my home-economics teacher. She taught her students how to plan and prepare economical meals, along with proper table manners. Often when the town fathers wished to eat a dinner before evening meetings, Miss DeWeese's students prepared and served it. It was excellent training. We were also expected to keep the home-economics building clean. In addition, we spent a portion of the year sewing, but that was not Miss DeWeese's forte, so we were given fewer instructions when fashioning garments. Still, we scheduled "fashion shows," to model our garments.

During my sophomore year I was elected district president of the Future Homemakers of America (FHA) owing to Miss DeWeese's encouragement. She drove me to Jackson, Tennessee, site of the district meeting, at which I was elected.

My English teacher was Mr. Skiles, an unmarried young man who had graduated *summa cum laude* from Vanderbilt University. Obion School was his first teaching position. He taught grammar and introduced us to good literature. He was especially determined that we understand

Shakespeare. His patience with us rural greenhorns paid off, at least with some of us, for my addiction to learning and reading older literature became a lifelong passion.

Music and singing have always appealed to me. When a gentleman who was a member of an orchestra in an adjoining county, volunteered his time to form a chorus from among the high-school students, I was overjoyed. He came once weekly for practice. The chorus not only performed concerts each year locally, but we consistently won second place in the annual Field Day program, at which all the county schools and one city school competed in singing and other categories. We felt it a special honor to place second, considering there were a number of trained voices among the city school chorus, which always took first place; whereas, not one of our chorus members had ever had the first lesson!

Once, our director asked me to sing a solo. I felt so inadequate I was literally petrified and so nervous my voice only squeaked the first time he asked me to go on stage and practice. Then he took me aside and kindly encouraged me, saying, "You can do it, Miss Yates; you can do it."

And I did! I sang "Danny Boy."

* * *

During those years it was quite common for students in rural schools to take a special trip somewhere near the end of their senior year. Only a few of the students had ever been outside our local county. The class as a group earned money to finance the trip throughout their high-school years. All the townspeople supported these efforts. One of our fundraisers was staging a play. In our junior-year play, I performed as the main character, Candy, a teenage girl. Our audience enjoyed it so much we were asked to give an encore performance. We made history, as no Obion School class had ever done so before. The same people and others attended that second performance and added several hundred dollars to our trip coffer.

We planned a trip to New Orleans by vote of the class. Though the express train to New Orleans passed through Obion, it never stopped there. However, our class sponsor, Mrs. Jack Berry (nee Amanda DeWeese), arranged for the train to stop for our class of 14 and our sponsor. The entire town turned out at the station to wave goodbye to us!

Mrs. Berry had also arranged for us to have many opportunities in New Orleans. Among them: a bus tour around the city by day and one by night, which included a visit to a gambling casino; a dinner in the French Quarter, where the entire menu was in French; and a dinner cruise on the *Andrew Jackson*. All these experiences were new and fascinating to me! However, I felt quite uncomfortable passing through the casino and clung tightly to the arm of a male classmate, hoping no one would report me to the elders back home for having entered a gaming establishment, possibly resulting in some kind of church discipline from them upon my return!

* * *

Though I worked almost daily, either part time or full time, I continued to earn high marks in all subjects throughout high school. At the end of my senior year, my average grade was the highest, so I became the valedictorian of my class.

Mr. Skiles volunteered to help me prepare and memorize my graduation speech. After I'd read through it a few times, he directed me to stand on the stage and recite the speech, making sure I pronounced every word correctly. He underlined certain words or phrases I should emphasize, and I practiced until I had it memorized. It was due to Mr. Skiles' faithful assistance that I managed to present it flawlessly at graduation. In addition, I was one of our senior quartet that sang "Among My Souvenirs," as part of our graduation program.

FRIENDS AND SWEETHEARTS

The very first day of school I met another freshman, Betty Jane "BJ" Foster, and we became best friends throughout high school. We often spent the night with each other. BJ was a Christian and taught me much about living the Christian life, for she had been brought up in the church since childhood and held strong convictions. We made senior pictures together after the individual class pictures were finished.

Following high school, our paths took us in different directions; and we lost contact for a number of years. However, in recent years we were able to renew our friendship and remain in touch, mostly via telephone, for we live in distant states.

* * *

My first boyfriend was a young man I met soon after the move to Obion. We sometimes rode bicycles together around the town. He was quite a handsome youngster, just a bit older than I. His family moved away soon afterward, and so ended our youthful affair.

Between work and school, I soon knew everyone in Obion, and I dated a number of young men during high school – even receiving one proposal of marriage from a man who was nine years my senior; but the one who stole my heart was Adam ____, the son of a prominent business family in a nearby town. We dated for almost three years, and I still have a little cedar chest, with our names engraved inside, dated 1949.

I think his parents might have encouraged our courtship more if I had lived in a better and bigger house and moved in higher social circles – there was a wide chasm separating our social classes. In any case, past high school, I had only one date with Adam. He called one day during the year I was attending MSC and asked if he could come to Memphis to see me.

When I answered, "Yes, he asked if I would arrange with two of my friends to go on a blind date with two of his friends, whom he wished to bring along.

I had two good friends at the boarding house where I was living, and they agreed to go.

Our dates treated us to a fine dinner, after which we went to see a touching movie about the trials and tribulations of a minister's family. (Was it an omen of my future?) My friends were pleased with their dates, for all three young men were perfect gentlemen, as Adam ever was. He walked me to the door and gave me a goodnight kiss, my last one from him. When I arrived home on my next visit, I learned he had married another! I never heard, nor did I ask, whether the wedding was the grandiose social event his parents had doubtless envisioned.

I never saw Adam again, except a few times in my dreams, and I know almost nothing of his subsequent life but was told he and his family established residency in another state.

Sometime later, one of Adam's relatives with whom I was acquainted came to me when I was back in Obion for a visit and said she and others among Adam's relatives loved me and had always thought I would become a part of their family clan. Belated consolation!

SPECIAL EVENTS

During my junior year, Miss DeWeese married, having fallen in love with Jack Berry, the son of a local politician. She asked three of her students, of whom I was one, to participate in her wedding ceremony, which took place in her parents' home in South Fulton, KY. What an exciting and special privilege!

Kate, governess of "Baby Herbert," stopped regularly by Little Victory Café. One day she came in and told me there was a contest in progress, sponsored by the *Memphis Press Scimitar*, to find the girl with the sweetest face in Tennessee to become the face of Nancy O in Andy Capp's comic strip "Lil Abner." Interested contestants were asked to submit a picture of themselves for judging. Kate requested a picture of me so she could enter it in the contest. I gave her one and, much to my surprise, my picture appeared soon in the *Memphis Press Scimitar* with the caption, "Sweetest Face in Tennessee."

One particular memory of my high-school years is indelibly printed on my heart. Each year the school held a beauty revue and selected a king and queen for the grammar school and a queen for the high school. The high-school queen was crowned Miss Obion, making her eligible to enter the annual Strawberry Contest at Humboldt, TN which concluded with the selection of a Strawberry Queen, who was then eligible to compete in advanced beauty revues.

A number of people asked me each year to enter the contest, but I steadfastly refused. It never occurred to me that I was an attractive young lady. Nor did I own an evening gown, and my finances did not provide money for one – or the necessary accessories.

When I was asked to enter the contest my senior year, my answer was no different.

However, the high-school student who was compiling the list of contestants, kept asking me, even begging me, to enter. I continued to refuse until a PTA mother broke down my defenses.

"Miss Yates," she said, "One of my daughters is getting a new gown this year for the beauty contest, and you may have the one she is discarding, if you are willing to enter the contest."

I consented, though I still harbored reservations.

The lady soon handed the gown to me. It showed quite visibly its many years of wear – the satin trim around the bottom was especially frayed. My name was already printed on the program, so I felt I had no choice.

The night of the contest, three judges sat at the edge of the stage; each contestant had to walk around the stage and face the judges, so they could take a closeup look. When my turn came to face the judges, I could not help hearing one of them remark, "Isn't she a beautiful girl? Look at her pretty teeth. But, oh, that ragged gown!"

I returned backstage, embarrassed and humiliated and practically in tears, determined never to go on the stage again. On the second round the top 10 were chosen. I heard my number (5) called among them but stood frozen.

Mrs. Berry, who organized the young ladies and assisted them during the contest, said, "Ruby, your number is being called."

"I don't want to go on stage again."

She said, "Yes, you are going," and she continued to insist.

I didn't budge.

She came toward me and literally pushed me back out onto the stage.

Much to my surprise, my number was called each succeeding round, and I was crowned Miss Obion that evening, with a handmade crown covered with aluminum foil! It became a keepsake and remained in my possession for many years.

Becoming Miss Obion brought several privileges, in addition to an invitation to the Strawberry Festival. The event I relished most was riding around in a shiny red convertible at the horse show held on the fairgrounds in Union City and having the privilege of presenting a handsome trophy to the winner of the horse show!

In short order, I received an invitation to the Strawberry Festival, along with tickets for all the events of the day and the proper attire required for each one.

The manager of Salant and Salant, Inc., my sponsor, soon appeared at my workplace and eagerly offered support. "Miss Yates, as your sponsor, Salant and Salant will see that you have the proper attire to attend the Strawberry Festival if you would like to go."

I didn't accept his offer, for I thought it would be accepting charity, and Mother had always taught me to do without what I could not afford – and never to accept charity; nor was I to envy those who possessed things I did not have.

I belatedly came to appreciate the offer of such generosity, for the clothing and accessories for the three major events at the festival – dresses for both a morning parade, during which I would ride on the queen's float, another one for the afternoon tea, and an evening gown for the beauty contest – would have required a tidy sum of money, and I owned nothing remotely suitable for any one of the occasions.

In retrospect, I know the sponsor's offer was sincere; I have sometimes wondered whether I should have accepted it, for it might have been twice a blessing, bringing joy to me and giving my sponsors the pleasure of helping someone of such little means. Also, I have wondered what chance I might have had to become the Strawberry Queen among the many beauties who entered the competition that spring of 1951.

MEMPHIS DAYS (1951-52)

Both BJ and I wanted to attend Freed-Hardeman College at Henderson, Tennessee at the same time, but I lacked the necessary funds. The school offered a valedictory scholarship, but it was too small for my needs. We were sad to be separated, but I hoped to join her later, just as soon as I had the necessary finances arranged. As it turned out, before I could enroll, BJ dropped out of school after the first quarter of her second year to marry a fellow student.

I made plans to attend Memphis School of Commerce (MSC) instead, in hopes I could quickly acquire the skills necessary to earn money to attend Freed-Hardeman later. The MSC representative who counseled me said I could pay a monthly fee, or a flat fee of $500 in advance, and continue in school as long as I wished; also, I could re-enter the school at any time thereafter for refresher courses, take new courses, or familiarize myself with any new technology that might be developed, at no additional cost. I opted for the latter choice, but getting the money remained a problem. My savings were insufficient to cover the cost of school plus living expenses.

Mother was supportive of my plans, but she had no money to assist me. I decided to approach one of the church pillars, a retired gentleman among Obion's upper crust of society. Mother walked with me to his house. He joined us on his front porch, where I explained my circumstances and asked if I might secure a loan of $500 from him.

He quickly replied, "No," followed by, "All the people who have borrowed money from me in the past never repaid it."

Unperturbed, Mother and I left his house and walked down town to see Mr. Emery Watson, president of Obion's only bank. I approached him about borrowing $500, explaining my intentions.

He hesitated not one moment. "Of course, Miss Yates, you may borrow the money. Just come into my office." Within a few minutes, the money was transferred into my account.

In August off to Memphis I rode, making the 100-mile trip via Greyhound bus, to enter MSC.

For the next nine months, I studied shorthand, advanced typing, business English, business math, the use of comptometers, and a couple of other business-related subjects.

THE BOARDING HOUSE

A long with eight or 10 other young women, I boarded for the first few months in a small, ordinary residential dwelling near MSC (long since closed). Some were students; others already had jobs in the city. The house was hot and stuffy during the late summer. A common refrigerator was provided for the residents to keep lunch food, but the only meal served was dinner each evening. I quickly learned to take moderate portions of whatever was passed around, for the dish was always empty once everyone had been served, and no second helping was offered.

Late one evening, the other girls invited me out for some "fun." We walked to a nightclub, where one girl proceeded to remove a bottle of whiskey from her bag and pass it around the table. Everyone took a swig or two – except me. About midnight we left for home, but some young men drove by, stopped, got out of their car, and started talking to the girls walking ahead of me. Whatever conversation ensued, the men soon returned to their car and drove away. I was thankful the group never again asked me to go out with them, for I had already determined what my answer would be.

Uncle R.P. Yates attended my graduation and brought me a used typewriter as a graduation gift, which served me well for practice. Each time I practiced my typing assignment at the crowded boarding house, it was necessary to shift something around on the small table I shared with a roommate. When not in use, I placed the typewriter at the foot of my bed, the only spot available. My roommate stepped on the space bar one day and broke it in two. She offered no apology at all but rather muttered some uncomplimentary remark indicating it shouldn't have been in her way.

After only a few months, I was blessed to discover an opening in a huge two-story house near downtown, which had earlier belonged to an aristocratic Memphis family but was later converted into a boarding house for young women. Both more spacious and less expensive than the first one, it provided a self-service light breakfast in addition to a commercial refrigerator for storing lunch provisions. No weekend food was provided, but those who did not travel home were welcome to prepare their own meals in the huge kitchen on first floor. Only occasionally did I travel home on weekends, for it was less expensive for me to remain in the city.

There I made good friends – two in particular – both of whom were young women. We sometimes walked downtown on Saturdays, ate a 50-cent lunch of two hamburgers, a piece of chocolate pie, and a soft drink at a Krystal café, after which we took a long walk on the esplanade along the eastern bank of the Mississippi River. On Sunday we usually attended our separate places of worship, but at least once or twice we also visited each the other's congregation and then freely discussed our differing beliefs.

Once while living there, I learned an elderly gentleman from the congregation in Obion had been admitted to a hospital in Memphis. I took a bus on Saturday morning to visit him. I stood at the foot of his bed and remained only for a brief visit, but I have never forgotten the penetrating look he gave me as I left, along with the following comment, "Miss Yates, if I am any judge of a person's character, you will do all right in life."

I know he was sincere, and it has been comforting to remember him and the others who spoke encouraging words to me along my sometimes-difficult pathway through life.

MY FIRST OFFICE JOB

Savings left from my high school work and the summer following graduation were being quickly depleted. I knew I must soon have additional money. On my own I secured work for the two-week Christmas holiday in a downtown retail store before taking the bus home to spend a weekend with Mother. As soon as I returned to MSC, I visited the school office and reminded the president of the promise to assist me in securing part-time employment when I needed money.

True to promise, MSC soon made arrangements for me to work in the downtown office of a cleaning supply business. I continued taking morning classes and worked afternoons for the duration of my time at MSC.

I took orders over the telephone and typed customer invoices. At first, I was nervous and made several typing errors. I even momentarily wished sometimes I could still be back in the cotton fields of home, where I felt completely comfortable! However, my boss was sympathetic with me and never complained about the precious time I wasted correcting errors. As a result, I gained confidence and soon began to feel comfortable and became efficient and began to enjoy my "on the job" training.

A BOOKKEEPER IN
NASHVILLE (1952-53)

Near the end of April, I received a call from Wade, who owned a Perma Shade awning business in Nashville and rented office space from Nashville Tent and Awning Company. He asked if I were interested in becoming bookkeeper for Nashville Tent and Awning, as the company was losing its current bookkeeper to marriage. The opportunity seemed to be a Godsend. I moved to Nashville and began work immediately, while the bookkeeper was still there to train me. I received two weeks' training from her before she left.

Situated on First Street, following the west side of the Cumberland River, Nashville Tent and Awning was owned by a second-generation family business. Three Husband brothers had inherited it from their father. The building was two stories, with offices both upstairs and downstairs. A large shop occupied the back of the first floor, where all kinds of tarpaulins, tents, truck covers, etc. were custom cut and sewn from heavy, waterproof canvas. My salary began at $45 a week and was soon raised an additional $5 – more money than I previously had earned ever in one week's time!

My duties included posting accounts receivable, sending out invoices and monthly statements, calling customers who were in arrears on payments owed (and sometimes having to give delinquent accounts to collection agencies or strike them off the books as uncollectible), making all deposits, keeping record of accounts payable, preparing and distributing employees' bi-weekly payroll (in cash), keeping petty cash available, preparing and filing all required state and federal reports; and keeping office supplies in stock.

My education, training and experience on various past jobs must have stood me in good stead, for before long I felt quite comfortable and enjoyed my work completely with one exception: calling those who had delinquent accounts, for it awakened me to the knowledge that some people are less than completely honest and accumulate debts they are less than diligent to repay.

My supervisor, Mr. Harry Husband, could not have been more respectful of me as a novice at office work; also, he was quite protective of me. He told me several times during my employment there I must never hesitate to hand over the company's money bag, should someone approach me on the street and demand it when I was on the way to the bank to make a deposit. He invited me to attend an Easter Cantata at which he sang beautiful solos at the church where he and his family attended. I appreciated the invitation and enjoyed the entire program.

SIBLING AFFECTION???

Wade arranged for me to board with my one of my older sisters, Lucille "Cille" Cothern, who had lived in Nashville since before she was married. Wade said he was sure Cille would charge me nothing for board – or, at most, no more than $5 a week. By the time I arrived, however, her price had gone up to $12 a week – $4 a week more than I had paid at the boarding house in Memphis!

Each time she added my clothes to her wash, she'd charge me an additional 75 cents. Also, each month she handed me checks to pay her bills at various locations around the city. It always took my entire lunch hour, sometimes two, at my fastest walking pace, to hand-deliver the monies.

Not only that, but I recall the time a benevolent neighbor who lived across the street called me over, soon after my arrival in Nashville, and gave me a handsome new pair of navy-blue leather dress pumps. She said the shoes didn't fit her well, but she thought I might like them. They were a perfect fit, and I was so proud of them. Unfortunately, I never got to wear them, because Cille met me at the front door as I returned.

"Let me try them on, Ruby."

I complied.

Her next words were "They fit me. You don't want them, do you?"

I did not answer her question; I just handed them to her.

In pondering the incident later, I realized this neighbor and I didn't wear the same size shoe, which led me to believe she bought them for me, a lass fresh from the country. Wishing to save me embarrassment, she simply said the shoes didn't fit her. I would feel bad to this day, had I ever learned that "Good Samaritan," was told I didn't want/like those attractive dress shoes.

Soon after moving to Nashville, I became baby sitter for Wade and Mildred's young son, Randy, my handsome little nephew with his natural coif of brown curly hair and an innocent infectious smile – altogether a lovable little chap. Once, they asked me to keep him for an entire weekend so they could go out of town. I had already made plans to visit Mother – it was one of my long weekends - so little Randy must accompany me. He sat quietly beside me on the Greyhound bus.

Randy accompanied me to Sunday morning worship and became curious when communion was served. He edged up close to me and asked, "Aunt Wooby, it is good?"

For my services, neither Wade or Mildred ever offered me any pay; nor was I ever invited into their home for a visit during the year and a half I worked in Nashville.

* * *

Each day I rode the bus to work I kept seeing the same young woman, who was also on her way to work. Presently, we engaged in conversation. It wasn't long before she invited me to move into a furnished apartment with her. We planned to split rent, food, cooking, and all other expenses on a 50/50 basis. As it turned out, that arrangement cost a few dollars less each month than boarding with my relative!

The two of us roomed together for the remainder of my time in Nashville. The only problem that ever developed was that I cooked the evening meal every other day and washed the dishes as agreed. My roommate took her turn cooking, but she procrastinated on washing dishes until no clean dish remained from which to cook or to eat. I considered she was punishing herself and said nothing, though I would have preferred her to complete the job every other day, just as I did. Still, we got along quite well, and she soon attended church services with me regularly and blended well with the young people there.

As soon as I began my new position in Nashville, I not only paid all my living expenses, but began immediately to repay the $500 loan to the

Obion Bank and gave tithes to the church I attended in East Nashville every Sunday. I lived as frugally as a Spartan, often walking the three miles to work on pretty days to save bus fare. I carried my lunch each day and bought only the necessary clothes. I spent no money for recreation and had only occasional dates with young men. In this way I was able to repay the entire debt plus the interest accrued during my tenure in Nashville.

PAINFUL OBSTACLES

My high-school basketball injury plagued me still, so I had to be careful not to bend my right leg in a certain way, lest my knee give way. Late one afternoon following dinner, I was enjoying a relaxing few moments outside just before dark. A short distance down the street, I jumped from a low retaining wall, and that old basketball injury on my right knee gave way once more, causing excruciating pain.

My knee was swollen the following morning, and I was in much pain. I was unable to return to work the rest of the week. I didn't know it at the time, but it was an omen of what was to come in later years. I called my supervisor and explained my problem. He insisted I go see a doctor.

I did so and had my first-ever knee x-ray. The doctor told me I had sustained much damage to the knee, in addition to having no cartilage remaining. He advised surgery but added it might leave me with a stiff knee. I had no health insurance; I could scarcely afford to pay the doctor's bill, much less afford an operation! Instead I nursed my injury for a few days and hobbled back to work.

I was still limping when I went to see a gentleman at the Tennessee Department of Education about the problem with my knee, explaining the injury had occurred during an official basketball game my freshman year at Obion High School. I asked if there were any possibility of getting help to pay the medical expenses should I yield to the recommended surgery.

His response was a curt and definitive "No!" He signaled further, by standing up, it was time for me to leave.

I continued to live with intermittent pain and some limitation of activities.

* * *

Though I never saw a dentist as a youngster or owned a commercial toothbrush until I was 10, Mother taught all her children how to make toothbrushes. We broke an 8-to-10- inch twig from a sweetgum tree, washed it, and chewed on one end until it looked like a fan brush such as artists use. We then applied a bit of salt and soda with which to brush our teeth.

No one ever took note that I failed to shed one of my infant teeth. The permanent tooth intended to replace that stubborn baby tooth was forced to embed itself sideways, just inside the surface of the roof of my mouth.

The first time I visited a dentist in Nashville, the hidden tooth was discovered. The elderly dentist suggested the infant tooth should be extracted and the permanent tooth surgically exposed and eventually forced into the right position through the use of braces (appliances).

I knew the infant tooth would not last, so I took his advice. A dental surgeon performed the procedure. After I healed, the original dentist fitted me with appliances, stating within a year the permanent tooth should be in its intended position. I do not remember the cost of that painful surgery, but the old dentist set his fee at $200 and applied braces.

The dental office was only a few blocks from work, so I walked there on my lunch hour for each weekly appointment, at which time the aged dentist would increase the pressure on the wayward tooth in an effort to pull it into place. The process caused me great pain, but the tooth stubbornly refused to budge.

Before long, the old man began to ask me to come to his office every day at noon. He pretended to adjust the appliances but was soon locking his examining-room door each time I entered and placing his hands on various parts of my body, gently at first but for a little longer period each day. I became frightened and embarrassed at his "professional" conduct.

I was a young, naïve country lass and had been taught always to obey and respect my elders – those who possessed the title of doctor, above all. It took me a few trips to his office to make up my mind how to handle the troubling situation, for I soon realized he had no good intention in mind if I allowed him to continue taking liberties for which I definitely gave him no permission!

When I gained courage sufficient to do so, I went to his office on my lunch hour as usual and entered the examining room. Again, he proceeded to lock the door. Before he touched me, I told him to remove the braces from my mouth; there had been no movement of the wayward tooth whatsoever, in any case. He began to pat me and place his hands on me in new places, saying, "Honey, you're just upset. It'll be all right, honey."

"I've made up my mind," I informed him. "You're not helping my problem, and I will never come to this office again."

He continued to try to put himself in an uncompromising position, but I pushed him away – he was thin and wizened – and I didn't budge from my predetermined course. After forcing him to leave me alone, he became defiant and blurted out as I was leaving, "Then you will pay me the full price of $200!"

I had already paid him half of his charge. I replied, "I shouldn't have to pay anything; you have not helped me at all."

He kept repeating the demand in such a forceful way, as he finally unlocked the door to allow me to leave his office, I felt threatened.

That entire afternoon I was apprehensive but did not know what I should do. Finally, I decided to confide in my boss. I felt too humiliated to give a full account of my experiences, but I told him the dentist was angry with me and demanding full payment, even though he had not really helped me at all and I had informed him that day I would never visit him again.

Mr. Husband was sympathetic with my story and likely suspected the most embarrassing part of the story I could not bring myself to reveal. He advised me to pay the full price as demanded and be done with it, instead of risking more difficulty from an unprincipled man. I did so; but, looking back, I marvel at how I was able to do so, in addition to paying for the recent dental surgery, an unexpected doctor bill resulting from my reinjured knee, and still manage my routine living expenses and repay the $500 school loan, plus accrued interest, so quickly. God really stretched my income!

CHURCH AND SOCIAL LIFE

My entire time in Nashville, I attended all services of the Eastland Church of Christ where the beloved brother Dorris Billingsley served as minister. (He has long since died; the church is no longer in existence in that location.) When that respected and revered brother announced he was leaving for a position with a congregation in another part of the city, there was more than a little weeping among the entire congregation.

The first Sunday I attended Bible class and worship, Neita Shockney introduced herself to me with a kind, sweet, and welcoming smile. In our initial conversation, I learned Neita's family lived just a short distance down the street from me.

It was easy to develop a friendship with Neita which has endured to this day, though both of us are past 80 years old. I was unattached and Neita was engaged to Jim Estes and waiting for him to complete pilot's training in the Air Force so they could marry. Besides participating in all the young people's activities at the church, we took walks together and visited in each other's home. I have never forgotten the scintillating aroma rising from the huge pan of mincemeat her mother had cooking on the kitchen stove one day when I went for a visit.

There was a rather large group of active teenage congregants, who planned various social activities; I soon became part of their group. An older member of the church, brother Bacigalupo, "Brother Baci," never failed to place money in someone's hand to be used on expenses for any outing we planned. Also, he was always greeting and encouraging us. We went on scavenger hunts, enjoyed hamburger cookouts, horseback riding, etc. In addition, there were several young married couples who served as chaperones for various occasions. They seemed to enjoy these parties and outings as much as their younger charges.

HOPE RENEWED

While living in Nashville I learned there were loans and grants made to deserving West Tennessee students by the Gooch Foundation of Memphis. I applied and informed the organization of my circumstances and received an immediate reply with a request for me to come to Memphis for an interview.

The good people at the latter boarding house, in which I lived while attending MSC, allowed me to spend the night there without charge. I purchased a round-trip bus ticket to Memphis, left work on a Friday afternoon at 5, and arrived in Memphis at midnight.

The Saturday-morning interview went well, and I returned to Nashville that afternoon. Within a few days I received a letter stating the foundation had awarded me a $400 grant for my first year of college. It was an answer to my ardent prayers, and I immediately registered for Freed-Hardeman College, knowing the school would award me a valedictory scholarship in addition to the grant. I would also apply for part-time work.

I was debt free when I was ready to leave Nashville and had a savings of $220 when I received my final pay check from Nashville Tent and Awning Company. I had become familiar with all the company employees, who gathered to wish me luck and Godspeed as they said their goodbyes.

I had made several other friends in Nashville, who planned a good-bye-bye party for me and prepared an album of notes and letters in addition to other gifts. (I treasured the album most and left it, among other prized items, stored at Paragould, Arkansas, during the four years Joe and I later spent in Norway. Upon our return, however, almost everything – including our wedding album – had to be discarded, as they were too damaged by mold to be salvageable.)

I had never owned a vehicle and had practiced driving for short distances no more than once or twice, so my dear brother-in-law, Wallace Martin, came to Nashville to help me move. First, he drove me to Obion, to spend a few days with Mother before FHC's fall quarter began.

FREED-HARDEMAN
COLLEGE (1953-54)

Wallace also moved me, along with my few possessions, to Freed-Hardeman College on Sunday afternoon, the day prior to fall registration. He helped me unload my few boxes, for I had only one small piece of luggage. Within minutes he was ready to return home.

With a twinkle in his eyes, a smile on his lips, and a quick kiss on the cheek, he said goodbye and issued the following teasing admonition, "Ruby, I have hauled you all over the state of Tennessee. If you don't find a husband here who can take care of you, I give up on you, girl!"

Neither of us had any way of knowing how prophetic his words would be.

I never understood why I was assigned the only room in the dorm which accommodated three students instead of the standard two. Both roommates and I were compatible, though I became fast friends with only one of them. From the beginning, one remained aloof, but there was never a conflict between us.

An initial requirement was to pass a spelling test. Fortunately, I passed it on my first try, and my registration went more easily and with less frustration than I had expected, for I'd earlier determined my two chief interests were home economics and language. I registered for the basic courses required of all freshmen, regardless of major, plus a beginning home-economics course and a Bible course, compulsory for all students.

The evening following registration, the upperclassmen presented stage entertainment for incoming freshmen. The emcee was a third-year student named Joe Wayne Pruett. It was my first glimpse of the young man who would become my husband the following summer. At the time, I took no note of him and have no memory of any of the entertainment, except the one love song a young man sang while he strummed on his guitar. I had never heard the lyrics before or since, and I am inclined to think he may have composed it for that occasion. I do recall it was something about a young man's interest in a young lady who did not return his affection.

* * *

I quickly became partial to two of my professors, W. Claude Hall and C.P. Roland. Brother Hall had an intimidating reputation, not only for his expertise in the field of English grammar and his accurate articulation, but also because he expected, yea, demanded, improvement from all students who entered his classroom. I had heard so many tales about him I was fearful of studying under him. I need not have worried, for I soon felt comfortable in his classes and absorbed as much from his teaching as my small brain could retain.

At the end of the school year, I slipped into brother Hall's classroom, where he was sitting alone at his desk, and asked him to sign my yearbook. After I left the room and read what he wrote, I floated on a high cloud the remainder of the day. His words were: "I've had a great number of students come to school to me, but if I ever had a better one than you, I cannot now recall who it might be." Signed W.C. Hall, May 25, 1954.

Of brother Roland, I had heard that in addition to being sedate, he was a boring, dry, and humorless instructor, albeit a Bible scholar. However, I was instantly attracted to his teaching methods and was delighted to sit at his feet the entire school year. I increased in Bible knowledge and grew spiritually a great deal under his teaching and influence.

During the school year, Joe Pruett, with whom I was then going steady, had an appointment in Memphis for an eye examination, and he wanted me to accompany him. Though I was certain brother Roland would deny me permission, Joe insisted I at least ask for it. I went to brother Roland's office and made my request.

Without skipping a heartbeat, he replied, "Permission granted!"

I could not believe my ears.

On our return to Henderson, Joe's vision was still blurred from having his eyes dilated, so he asked me to drive part of the way as soon as we were outside the city limits of Memphis. I had seldom touched the steering wheel of a car and required some instructions from Joe, but I took the wheel and drove until we neared campus. Fortunately, there was little traffic along the rural route we took; surely our guardian angels looked out for us, because we returned without an accident or a ticket for my driving without a license!

On another occasion, a student came to the class I was attending with a note from brother Roland, asking me to come to his office. Brother Roland was a member of the discipline committee, which demanded strict limits of behavior and approved of certain activities only. All the way to his office, I kept thinking I surely must have unwittingly broken a rule, for which I should receive punishment.

Upon my arrival, brother Roland said, in his soft unobtrusive voice, "Miss Yates, I have to be away tomorrow. Would you teach my English class?"

Oh, what a blessed relief to my anxieties!

It was a grammar lesson, and I really didn't have any difficulty with the class, for I had covered nearly all the same material in my senior year of high school. I suppose I can say it was the first college class I ever taught, though in subsequent years I taught a great many during my 10 years as an adjunct instructor at Faulkner University's Birmingham campus.

I WORK FOR THE PRESIDENT

As soon as I was settled in my classes, I applied for part-time work. Apparently, he had investigated my background, for President H.A. Dixon asked me to do secretarial work for him 20 hours a week for the entire school year. I took the request in stride, but it occurred to me later he was getting a bargain: an experienced and efficient secretary for the price of 50 cents an hour!

My hours varied each day, and changed each quarter, depending on my class schedule. Each time I reported for work, President Dixon was always prepared to dictate several letters. If I had time remaining after I finished typing his correspondence, I assisted the college bookkeeper (posting accounts, filing, etc.), whose office adjoined the president's.

I paid no money to FHC during the year; neither was I paid for my secretarial services for President Dixon until the end of the school year. With the $400 Gooch Foundation grant, the amount allowed me as the honor student of my high-school class, and the funds earned for my year's secretarial work, FHC owed me money. I do not recall the amount, but it was probably worth waiting for, because by then I was making plans for a summer wedding and I needed the cash!

SIGMA RHO SOCIETY

There were no fraternities at FHC, but rather four societies; each student had opportunity to join the one of his/her choice. In addition to providing social activities, the various societies participated in competitive activities, including campus sports, debating clubs, chapel programs, etc. Hence, each society competed for membership.

I became a proud member of the Sigma Rho Society and participated in its activities as often as my schedule permitted. During the second quarter, a recruiting dinner was planned for high-school seniors, their sponsors and parents from Obion and surrounding counties of my home area. The Sigma Rho Society elected me to make a presentation at the meeting, representing the college, Sigma Rho Society as well. I was expected to speak about my experiences at FHC and tell why I would recommend it to other students. I accepted the honor with reflective reservations, for I remembered how my knees always shook during high school when I had to make an oral report or stand before an audience in any capacity.

On the evening of the occasion, there sat my favorite high-school teacher in whose wedding I had participated, Mrs. Jack Berry. She had chaperoned several prospective students from Obion School. Following the meal, I was introduced and began my presentation. All went satisfactorily until I froze midway in the speech for what seemed an eternity. Finally, I recovered my voice and completed my remarks, albeit with great embarrassment.

Upon my return to campus that night, I quietly prayed about my problem and asked God to help me become a public speaker. I promised God I would do my best, even if it took me an entire lifetime. I could hardly wait to enroll in a beginning speech class in which preparation was begun to keep my commitment to God and myself.

God granted me the strong determination to succeed at my objective. Though it took years, in time I overcame such profound timidity stemming from childhood; and I possess documents, which prove I attained my goal. In subsequent years I became not only a secondary and post-secondary teacher, but I taught ladies' Bible classes for more than 30 years. I was the featured speaker for many ladies' religious programs and retreats in Alabama, Tennessee, and Texas. I have given various secular and civic talks. Once, I had the honor of speaking about friendship at Birmingham's elite social club, The Club, at the request of a dear friend, Joyce Vinsant, whose daughter was honoring friends in connection with her upcoming marriage. In addition, I was one of three teachers selected by the Alabama Department of Education to conduct training classes in Decatur for Alabama teachers on how to incorporate career ideas into all teaching units, regardless of subject matter.

With my permission years later, some of my career units were sent to the U.S. Department of Education in Washington DC. A friend of mine, who was an Alabama State Supervisor of Education at the time, chastised me for not having my work copyrighted to earn money. Such a thought never entered my mind. I recall the brilliant and gifted Madame Curie, who in concert with her husband, discovered radium. Instead of applying for a copyright, she declared it an element which belongs to the entire world. I claim no kinship to those brilliant and gifted people, but I was glad to share my work with all who might benefit from it.

SOCIAL LIFE AT FHC

Some young people shunned attendance when they learned about FHC's strict rules of social behavior and other limitations imposed upon students. For example, social hour was from 6-7 p.m. each day, and nothing more than holding hands was permitted on campus. Past the seven o'clock hour, students were to be in their rooms or in the library studying until lights out, promptly at 10 p.m. Double dating in cars was permitted only after the school received written permission from parents granting such privilege. Students caught breaking the rules were called before the discipline committee for punishment, which sometimes led to expulsion, depending upon the seriousness of the infraction.

Though I had already lived independently for years before entering FHC, I had no difficulty complying with the rules; however, I was fully aware some students broke them. Once, friends of a couple I had often seen "smooching" in a not-too-private nook accused me of reporting the kissing couple to the discipline committee. They refused to believe me when I said I had never reported anyone. Other than Professor Roland, I had no knowledge of who made up the discipline committee.

According to tradition, dating during social hour became a popular pastime, and so many sweethearts were going steady, often followed by the announcement of engagement, that one might think FHC was running a marriage bureau. An upper classman asked me for a date soon after my arrival on campus. After a couple of weeks, he asked if I would go steady with him, but I declined. He seemed like a perfectly fine young man, but I had no desire for our relationship to go beyond friendship.

Only a few weeks later, a friend of Joe's from his hometown of Paragould, Arkansas, began coming to me daily with an oblique message from Joe. It was about two weeks before the messages became clear to me: Joe wished to date me!

Joe's mediator explained: Joe had worked for a congregation in Texas the previous summer and had become "almost engaged" to the daughter of the minister's family there. He had, in fact, left his high-school class ring with her, but now wished he could take it back, freeing him to date others.

Ultimately, I told the young man if Joe wished to date me, he would have to speak for himself.

Once my message was delivered, Joe lost no time in hurrying over to the girls' dormitory to talk with me during social hour. He asked me not for one date but for several before he returned to his own student residence.

There was another residual issue. Joe had dated another young lady at FHC the previous year. I can only theorize from what happened soon afterwards that she was interested in resuming their courtship. In any case, before my first date with Joe was fulfilled, two of her friends, also upperclassmen, burst into my room and informed me – in no uncertain terms – I was not to date Joe, for he and their friend, who had dated the previous school year, were still attracted to each other.

"I have no intention of stealing any girl's boyfriend. I did not approach Joe for a date; it was he who approached me," was my response. I think her friends left my room a bit crestfallen.

* * *

FHC made preaching arrangements for advanced ministerial students. Soon Joe had a preaching appointment at the Obion congregation, and he asked whether I would like to accompany him there. I was delighted to do so, for it gave me opportunity to spend the day with Mother.

I took Wallace aside that day and reported I had my eyes on someone who might be able to "haul me around" in the future; and, if so, I would relieve him of that duty!

Joe's weekend appointments were often in an area near his hometown, and he sometimes invited me to go home with him on those weekends. When I was able to accept his invitation, I usually stayed with "Granny

Higgins," his maternal grandmother, who lived in a small apartment in Paragould, AR. She was always accommodating, friendly, and kind, and did her best to make me feel comfortable.

Prior to the Christmas holidays, Joe began quizzing me about when I planned to ask him to marry me. I considered he was teasing and laughed at the idea without response. He persisted.

After he made the query several times, I said emphatically, "If I have to ask you to marry me, there will be no wedding; for I have no intention of doing so!"

He understood that message well, for that very evening he proposed to me. I cannot recall all the feelings I had at that time, subconsciously realizing what a change was about to transpire in my life. I remember distinctly, however, when we parted, I went to my room and read Proverbs 31 about the virtuous woman.

In the meantime, Joe had written his Texas girlfriend and asked her to return his ring. I never knew exactly what he said in that letter, but she obliged his request. I felt only sympathy for her when Joe told me afterward he had known all along she had cared more for him than he cared for her.

Joe spent the Christmas holidays with his parents; I spent mine with Mother. Joe presented me with a small diamond engagement ring and a cedar chest. His funds must have been as limited as mine, for neither was paid for until after we were married! And it was February of the following year before I was able to give him a belated gift of four volumes of religious commentaries, *Barnes Notes*, paid for in full!

Following the holidays, both of us returned to campus and settled into the second quarter. Joe preached somewhere almost every weekend, and we began to make plans for a simple summer wedding.

Joe dropped out of school at the end of the second quarter, so he could repair some of his family's discarded furniture for our use; after more than 60 years, we are still using two of the family dressers he refinished while applying to congregations needing a minister whose members were willing to work with a young beginner.

The Lord blessed him, for he soon received an invitation to preach for the congregation in Thayer, Missouri, in the foothills of the Ozark Mountains. The city was located on U. S. Highway 63, just across the border from Mammoth Spring, Arkansas, site of the giant underground Mammoth Spring, which perpetually erupts with great force.

I remained at FHC the entire school year, then hurried home to complete preparations for our June 13 wedding.

PRE-NUPTIAL PARTIES

The ladies of the Obion congregation hosted a special wedding tea/ shower for me in the home of Becky Board, wife of one of Obion's businessmen. The party consisted of two parts, one during the afternoon and one during the evening, in order to accommodate those women who worked at one of the two Obion shirt factories. Though I had given no thought to the selection of a china or crystal pattern, the one local jeweler was somehow alerted; she yanked me into her store as I walked by one day and insisted I make selections. For china I chose Apple Blossom by Haviland, and for crystal I chose Century by Fostoria.

Many of the guests pooled their gift money to buy a single piece of china or crystal. Altogether, I received eight place settings of china and eight crystal glasses, plus a few basic serving pieces.

I treasured every piece and have cared for them lovingly, though I was unable to use them during our first years of marriage. However, in later years I have used it all with pride and a thankful heart, always taking pleasure in telling guests who gave it to Joe and me so long ago. Rarely have we had to replace a piece or two, due to accidental breakage; and I have been able to add a few additional pieces to the original sets.

After the tea, Mrs. Board sent Mother all the left-over party foods, enough of everything for the wedding reception. (I suspect she had this in mind when she purchased supplies, to relieve Mother of most of the reception expenses – which she could ill afford.)

With massive food contributions, Mother had only to purchase a three-tiered cake from a bakery in Union City for $12.50! (I still have the bride and groom that adorned its top layer.) Joe drove with one of my brothers-in-law the 17 miles to Union City, early on Sunday morning, the day of the wedding, to pick up the cake and returned in time for morning worship.

Joe's Aunt Irene Higgins hosted a shower for me in her home in Paragould. I received some practical and useful gifts at that party. I also received a few gifts from friends in Nashville.

At neither party did I receive a rolling pin, so at my first opportunity, I bought a second-hand one made of solid hardwood for $1.50. Since then, I have rolled out many thousands of biscuits, cookies, and pastries; but the rolling pin shows almost no wear and will surely last for many more generations, if it receives proper care.

My sister, Clodine Martin, hosted the rehearsal dinner in her spacious home and prepared the meal, for Mother's house was too small to accommodate the entire wedding party.

THE WEDDING

My wedding dress was a simple tea-length white cotton eyelet dress, suitable for any afternoon tea or other dressy occasion; my shoes were white leather pumps with two-inch heels. The tiara was homemade and given to me.

The wedding party consisted of a maid of honor, a friend from college days; my young nephew, Wilton Martin, served as my usher. I first asked dear brother B.T. to give me away, but shyness prevented his doing so; brother-in-law Wallace stood in as my father. Joe's best man was his brother-in-law, Joe Corley; his usher was Norman Fultz; both men were friends from college days at FHC. Joe's cousin, Winston Burton, officiated.

All music was performed *a cappella*, including the "Wedding March." A quartet made up of local young men of my acquaintance sang wedding songs. All the vocal music was lovely and melodious, especially the solo, "Eternally" rendered by one member of the quartet who had experienced years of voice training.

The wedding was scheduled to begin on Sunday afternoon at 4, allowing minister Joe Corley time to drive to Obion from Marvel, Arkansas, where he was determined to preach for the morning worship at his congregation there. He arrived 30 minutes late on that sweltering, 110-degree June afternoon, due to a delay in traffic at Millington, TN, where the local naval base was hosting an air show. There was nothing to do but wait in sultry heat sans air conditioning! I sat in a classroom behind the vestibule and stared through an open window facing the street, hoping every passing car would be Joe Corley's. In the meantime, I began to drip with perspiration, resulting in a completely wilted hair style. No doubt, the wedding guests were perspiring also and wondering if indeed a wedding would take place after all.

Though delayed, the wedding proceeded without further incident. Afterward, the guests traveled the short distance to Mother's house for the reception, where they were served refreshments to enjoy as they meandered their way throughout the house to view the wedding gifts I had on exhibit wherever I could find a spot.

When news of Joe Corley's delay reached FHC, Professor Roland mistakenly understood it was the *groom* who arrived late, not the best man, he commented, "I always knew Joe Pruett was slow, but I thought that boy would at least arrive on time for his wedding!"

THE HONEYMOON

A few weeks prior to our wedding, someone in my family received a letter from my older sister, Beulah Kingrey of Chicago, stating her WWII-veteran husband, Jack, was gravely ill and nearing death. She pleaded for a visit from someone in the family. The letter was circulated throughout the family, but all of them insisted they could not afford to make the trip.

"Ruby and Joe are planning a honeymoon trip," a family member belatedly suggested. "Why can't they travel to Chicago?"

When I was approached about the proposed trip, I contacted Joe, who agreed. As soon as the reception ended, we left for Chicago in Joe's old car. Our friends had written on the back window, "Just Married" on one line and "Watch Thayer, Missouri Grow!" on a second line. In addition, they had placed several rocks inside each hubcap, which made a terrible noise with each revolution of the tires; it was the following day before we could find a service station with someone willing to remove the hubcaps and discard the rocks.

Our wedding night was spent in a not-so-desirable motel in Cairo, Illinois, along the way, the only one in which we could find lodging, for Joe had made no previous reservations. We arrived in Chicago the following day, in time to pay a visit to Jack, who was barely holding on to life in his hospital bed; he was able to converse with us briefly. We made two additional visits before beginning our return trip. Beulah notified us a few days later of Jack's death.

On our return trip, we stopped in Fulton, Kentucky, for a brief visit with Aunt Lona, then spent a night with Mother before proceeding to our new home in Thayer. Upon arrival on Friday afternoon, we drove directly to the small, four-room house which would be our home for the next 15 months. Joe lifted me into his arms and carried me across the threshold. He wore a grin on his face, but I thought he was privately wishing I weighed fewer pounds! Our first meal that evening consisted of a can of soup and soda crackers.

THAYER, MISSOURI (1954-55)

An Unusual Welcome

About 9 that first evening, we heard a loud noise and a banging at our front door. When we opened it, the entire congregation, or so it seemed, marched through the house and out the back door, making "music" on boards, tin cans, and various other noisemakers, ignoring us completely. They repeated the action three times, leaving a sack of unlabeled canned goods on the kitchen counter with each round.

As they entered a fourth time, several of the men brought in a huge log several feet long and told Joe to hop onto it. He obeyed and they started out the door with Joe astride the log. One brother turned around to face me and explained they intended to dump Joe into the underground Mammoth Spring. He assured me I shouldn't worry, as they had used a bale of hay to test how long it would take for one to resurface – only three days! And away they went.

The ladies remained with me and did their best to keep me entertained with many tales about the area and the congregation. About midnight, the gang returned with Joe still safe and sound. They left immediately after a few laughs, but not before one dear sister came up and whispered into my ear that not all of the canned food contained food for human consumption. She suggested I should be on the lookout for dog food. I had never seen any kind of commercial dog food in my life, for our family's pets received only kitchen refuse and table scraps.

I remembered the dear sister's warning; and every time I opened a tin, I cautiously looked at the contents, to determine whether it contained something I couldn't identify. If it did, I knew it must be dog food. I was so thankful she had warned me; otherwise, Joe and I would likely have consumed the six or seven cans of dog food contained in our welcoming shower.

We stored our food in the cabinets and opened only one can a day, so the supply lasted several months. Each one usually provided us with something suitable for a lunch, except one day when I had to open four cans in succession, for the first three contained coconut.

After everyone left, Joe told me the men had actually taken him to the head of the spring and threatened to cast him into it before bringing him home. When at last we went to bed, we discovered someone had tied tin cans containing rocks to every slat under the mattress, which Joe removed the following day. I had read some English literature and concluded this night's initiation was the Thayer brethren's version of the English shivaree of olden times.

LIVING ARRANGEMENTS

The brethren had agreed to pay Joe a $50 weekly wage, and they arranged for us to live in a small, fully furnished four-room house, which had belonged to an aged couple whose children rented it after their parents' deaths. Once a month, $10 was deducted from the week's salary to help with the rent. The house was ideal, since we owned only three pieces of furniture – two old discarded but refinished dressers and the cedar chest Joe had given me the previous Christmas.

I recall how grimy and soiled the old gas stove was when we arrived, and I had not cleaned it properly before Mother visited us for a few days not many months after we married. She spent most of her time cleaning that stove! (One of Mother's "gifts" was keeping pots, pans, and her stove squeaky clean.) She liked doing it, but I was embarrassed and decided then she would never again come to our house and find a dirty stove. Since that day, I have kept my kitchen stove and oven clean, wherever we happened to live.

Many years later Joyce Vinsant, a friend in Birmingham, would occasionally ask when she came to visit, "Ruby, may I have a look at your clean and shining stove just to get some inspiration!"

ADJUSTMENTS

I suppose all marriages require a period of adjustment. Joe and I came from different backgrounds, as many couples do. Though his parents were not wealthy, he had not endured poverty as had I. While he had spent the first few years of his life in the country, he was a city boy with every fiber of his being. He manifested little enthusiasm for hunting and fishing, and completely detested picking cotton, gardening, berry picking, etc. – all the activities to which I had been born and bred as a youngster. The only two farm activities he preferred were horseback riding and driving a tractor. He often spent a day or two with his cousin in the country so they could drive tractors and perhaps ride on horseback to the rural schoolhouse on Friday evening to see a "picture show."

When I married, I missed Mother sorely. Perhaps because of our intimate relationship, marriage required more adjustments of me than Joe. Joe corrected my singing at first, followed by wondering aloud what he had done wrong when I burned the fried okra or fried chicken! On such occasions I would give no response, just run to the bedroom, fling myself across the bed, and weep.

Once I could compose myself and return to Joe's company, I would usually lament, "I wish I could see Mother!" Joe made no response.

Joe wore starched white dress shirts for all his ministerial duties. His parents had paid for them to be laundered professionally since he entered college. On his meager salary, we could not afford that luxury, so I did my best to prepare them properly, though I had never performed that chore prior to our marriage.

Once, when I finished ironing one of his shirts, Joe noticed I had pressed a crease on the right side of the front collar. He quickly pointed out my grievous error, followed by the admonition, "If you have to press a crease in the collar of my shirt, will you please place it at the back of the shirt from now on?"

Oh, how I hurried to the bedroom and wept for some time!

Upon my return, I repeated what he had already heard a number of times: "I wish I could see Mother."

This time Joe spoke emphatically, "If you do not quit announcing you want to see your mother, I'll take you home to your mother!"

Surely, he was bluffing???, but I think I grew up at that moment, and never again made such a statement, though I always missed Mother and found a way to visit her frequently as long as she lived. She died in 1991, and I miss her still and trust I'll meet her at heaven's gate.

I'm not sure I have mellowed much through the years, but Joe certainly has, and has long since ceased to criticize me in hurtful ways. Neither of us wears a mask, but we speak frankly with each other, as well we should. The two most troubling problems we have ever faced in our marriage occurred during our middle years. I think I took child rearing more seriously than Joe and was a much stricter disciplinarian; this sometimes led to conflict. The other serious problem had to do with Joe's blind faith in some untrustworthy persons, which led to financial struggles for us.

OUR WORK

Joe and I felt right at home with the church in Thayer from the very beginning. The congregation consisted of more than 100 members, including a large group of teenagers, and there was always work to do. We felt blessed to be used in the Lord's work. In addition to Joe's weekly Sunday sermons and teaching adult classes, he taught a weekly Friday-evening Bible class at a rural congregation a few miles outside Thayer. We visited the sick and shut-ins and others wherever a door of opportunity to help or teach opened. We sat up all night with people in the community who needed round-the-clock care and who would have been receiving critical care – perhaps hospice care – in today's society and conducted funerals and weddings. In addition, the ladies met regularly to sew quilts to be given to the orphanage at Morrilton, Arkansas.

Joe and brother Boyd Morgan, minister of the nearby Mammoth Spring, Arkansas, congregation, alternated in delivering a radio sermon each Sunday, for which our youth chorus sang live. We visited area meetings; Joe led the singing for many of them. He also conducted some protracted meetings for rural congregations in the area surrounding Thayer, in addition to teaching a two-week singing school at Hardy, Arkansas, during our second summer in Thayer.

Joe and I soon formed a quartet with another young couple in the congregation, Berry and Ruth Honeycutt. I was the only one with no formal training, but Joe taught me the soprano part, and together we represented all four parts. News travels fast, probably because Berry was a local bank official and knew everyone in the area. He could be free from the bank for some hours any time there was a need, and soon we were in demand to sing for funerals, a service we were happy to render.

We conducted a Vacation Bible School (VBS) during the summer of 1955. Joe and I received permission to taxi several children to it each day. If memory serves me correctly, on some days we transported as many as nine children in our small vehicle!

Most congregations among us sing a cappella in worship. One morning during the week of VBS, when all the children were singing together in the auditorium prior to attending class with their age group, a precious little girl seated beside me, one of the ones we brought with us to class every day, suddenly stopped singing, looked at me, and queried, "Miss Ruby, where is your piano?"

"We do not have one," I whispered.

Satisfied with my answer, she continued singing quite merrily.

The church flourished (and continues to do so). A few years ago, we had opportunity to visit the congregation when we traveled through Thayer. We were pleased to be re-introduced to three ladies at whose weddings Joe officiated while serving their congregation. We thanked God to learn the congregation has continued to experience such phenomenal growth, it required a larger facility. They sold their beautiful small stone building to another religious group, purchased acreage on U.S. Highway 63 Bypass, and built a much larger house of worship. When we visited, they were in the process of still further expansion.

COOKING SKILLS?

Learning to cook was a slow and sometimes embarrassing process. I was determined to be a hospitable minister's wife and often invited people into our home for a meal. I had worked all my life and knew how to do many things, but learning to cook, especially on a gas stove, was often a disastrous experience for me – and for our guests – though I put forth my best effort.

I remember distinctly the first time I fried chicken for Sunday dinner when Mom and Pop Pruett popped in unexpectedly. It looked a delicious crispy brown on the outside, but inside it was still raw; we could manage to eat only the outer portions.

Another time, someone brought fish and stayed to eat with us. I filled the skillet with pieces of fish when the cooking oil was barely warm and left the burner on low for the entire cooking process. Soon the fish pieces began to fall apart and became soggy with fat and had the consistency of grits. No one had an appetite for that meal.

Other culinary adventures were equally disastrous; eventually I became a satisfactory cook; some have described me as a very good cook, even an excellent one. I suppose that depends upon the guests' appetite and taste. I continue to invite people into our home regularly and can at least say I've had a great deal of experience.

Thinking back about all those inedible meals I attempted to prepare for Joe and the families of the Thayer congregation, I'm sure they discussed how horrible the dishes I set before them tasted and how they would decline a second invitation. They likely went home and prepared themselves a meal, for it was before the rise of fast-food restaurants on virtually every street corner; but I trust no one found fault with my efforts at being hospitable.

SPECIAL MEMORIES

Several activities remain outstanding in my memory. We quickly became attached to the large group of fine teenagers in the congregation and planned weekly activities for them. They returned our affection and were cooperative in every way. Our activities included games of croquet, scavenger hunts, cookouts, visits to neighboring congregations, and evening singings. We have never been among or worked with a finer group of young people.

Among the families we visited was a widow bedridden and in isolation with tuberculosis. We were told about her and informed no one visited her because of her contagious disease. Joe and I visited regularly and took lunch to her; sometimes it comprised just a small can of Vienna sausages and a vegetable or two, along with some cornbread. She always seemed grateful for whatever it was. She probably felt as sorry for us as we did for her, knowing we shared such as we had with her, knowing also how others shunned her.

Also, among those whom we visited regularly was an elderly couple who earlier had been active Christians but were then homebound. Any time we went by near mealtime, they never failed to ask us to stay and eat with them. They were poor, so we thanked them and offered an excuse. (Mother had taught me I might be taking food the family needed if I ate with our poor neighbors when I was growing up – even though our family was the poorest among them.) The old couple continued to invite us to eat with them every time we stopped by, and one late afternoon, we accepted their invitation. Our meal consisted of a can of pork and beans and fried cornbread patties. I have never forgotten the joy it brought to them – and to us – to share that meal together.

Another special memory was the time I hosted a wedding shower in our house for a young lady of the congregation. We had absolutely not one penny left to purchase a gift after I had prepared all the refreshments, so I reluctantly wrapped one of my treasured wedding gifts, a beautiful vase, as a present for the bride. One of the guests commented on the vase's beauty and asked whether I had purchased it locally. I responded "No," in a pinched voice, fearing my guest would ask more. She likely suspected its origins, owing to my reaction, for she asked no further questions. I was thankful, for my embarrassment would have surely surfaced to a greater degree, had I been forced to admit the truth about the gift.

"BROTHER JOE"/ "YOUNG MAN"

Working with the church at Thayer was one of sheer joy, love, and thanksgiving. We had the full support of everyone, with perhaps the exception of two brief incidents, which involved two quite elderly gentlemen. Even then, the other congregants assured us, we should consider the gentlemen's age and overlook what happened. We did so and nothing more came of either incident. I include them because, looking back, I recall them as not only unusual, but somewhat amusing – though at the time both caused me such anxiety I momentarily felt as though I should faint.

One gentleman had served a long term as an elder. When we moved there, he had outlived the other elders, but considered himself to be an elder for life and refused to resign. When Joe preached a sermon on eldership, he mentioned elders serve in plurality in the local congregation, according to Acts 14:23 and other scriptures, and by implication, therefore, one man should not serve alone. Before Joe had completed other scriptures which state that elders are to rule well, as they must give an account; nor should they lord it over God's heritage, among other things, the old gentleman who believed he was appointed an elder for life arose from his seat near the rear of the sanctuary.

"Brother Joe, who do you think is guilty of that around here?" he asked.

Joe stopped his sermon and looked directly at the old brother; after a few seconds' reflection, he responded, "Brother Drew, I always try to make my sermons apply to the audience in general, but I say, 'If the shoe fits, wear it!'"

At that moment, I had that sinking feeling I might faint, though I tried to remain calm. Nothing further was said, and Joe continued with his sermon as if nothing had happened.

Following the worship, everyone tried to console us, especially me. Although I had not been brought up in a Christian environment and was certainly unused to that kind of outburst, I had to learn through sometimes-painful experiences that Christians have imperfections too.

The other old gentleman was a retired railroad employee who always carried his huge railroad watch in his pocket. One day, he was sitting in a pew near the pulpit. When he judged Joe had preached long enough, he stood, pulled his watch from his pocket, turned around to make sure he had an audience, and then sat down.

Following worship, he went directly to where Joe was greeting congregants, pointed a finger in Joe's face, and in a sonorous voice made the following threatening comment, "Young man, if you want to preach here, you've got to learn to quit on time! We are railroad people here, and we do things on time!" The man's statement was partially true. Thayer served as a terminal for the Cotton Belt Railroad between Memphis and Kansas City, Missouri. It was recognized as a railroad town, and many Thayer residents were railroad employees.

After a few seconds' reflection, Joe responded, "Brother, I usually preached as long as it takes to complete my sermon, and some sermons are longer than others!

Again, I stood frozen until the love and sincere sympathy of the members enabled me to regain my composure. I am a keenly sensitive person, and it was only with subsequent experiences I learned to keep a calm demeanor when problems or critics arose within the church or elsewhere.

I do not recall whether Joe shortened his sermons at all thereafter, and we have experienced difficulties of a much more serious nature throughout the years; but we never have had any other incidents comparable to those two.

I EARN A PHT (1955-57)

The Thayer congregation grew, and our work brought us many joyous blessings. It was hard to think of leaving, but Joe expressed a strong desire to continue his schooling. FHC was a junior college at the time. Joe's commendable wish to earn a degree meant he must attend a college elsewhere. He chose another Christian one, David Lipscomb College (DLC), now David Lipscomb University, in Nashville.

We made a brief trip to Nashville during the summer of '55 where Joe enrolled for the fall term. My job was not to earn a college degree but rather a PHT; that is, Push Hubby Through, and I was more than willing to do my part. I applied to Southern Bell, took a math test, and was interviewed. The Company subsequently hired me just as soon as we moved to Nashville.

That fall we packed our few belongings and bade a tearful goodbye to our wonderful Christian family at Thayer and were soon on our way to Nashville. We are now past 80 years old, and Joe has preached in many states, Canada, and three of the four Scandinavian countries, but we have never lived among a more cooperative, loving group of people than the saints at Thayer. We hold the memory of our time there dear to our hearts.

HOUSING, SCHOOL, AND WORK

Joe and I first rented a one-room efficiency apartment in East Nashville for $45 a month, including utilities. The unit made up half of the upstairs of a small residential dwelling. A bed, chest of drawers, a small table, and two chairs became our living room, dining room, and bedroom. Our "kitchen" was a tiny anteroom furnished with a tiny stove and a small utility table. There was only room to stand and cook; I had to back out or carefully turn around to exit. One naked light bulb was strung from the ceiling in each area. There was a common bathroom at the end of the upstairs hallway.

Though our location was far from DLC and my job, we lived there until we had the opportunity to move into an ample downstairs apartment near campus for only $50 a month, including all utilities. Joe entered DLC within a few days of our move from Thayer and became a full-time student. We remained in our comfortable apartment until Joe had earned his B.A.

Joe had secured work preaching for the Gladeville congregation, a rural community about 25 miles from Nashville; he began preaching the first Sunday after our arrival in Nashville. The pay was $25 per Sunday.

In addition to his income from preaching at "The Glade," Joe worked at the post office during the Christmas holidays for both of our Nashville years. During the summer of 1956, between terms, he was employed by a church in Grenada, Mississippi, for $75 a week as a substitute minister, while their regular minister was away. We saw each other only once during that time, when I rode the "Greyhound" to Grenada for a weekend visit. We saved all this extra income to pay for his schooling and associated expenses.

Joe received no scholarship money or grants; nor did our families, the church, or anyone else provide us with funds. We worked out a budget that allowed us to pay all our living expenses and all school costs. Joe's earnings went toward his schooling, and my salary went toward living expenses, my transportation to work, car payment, food, rent, and church contribution. There was no thought of new clothes, entertainment or any kind of frills.

Those years were frugal, lean ones, albeit pleasant, and we have no regrets. We kept current on all expenses, with one exception: a $400 fee tacked onto the usual cost of one of Joe's final courses.

We sought a loan from a Thayer friend, Berry Honeycutt. We immediately received the money – with no loan document attached. We could have assumed it was a gift, but we repaid him promptly - just as soon as we were settled into Joe's new work at Trinity, Alabama, following his graduation.

There were no enhancements during those lean years or for many years afterward, but we managed financially on our own. I firmly believe the discipline demanded of us developed us into good money managers. Our children now tell us we have been good stewards of God's blessings, which have come our way in later years. Unfortunately, however, we have been vulnerable to less-than-honest people at times and have lost money more than once.

SCHOOL AND
WORK ROUTINE

Life quickly settled into a routine. The Glade brethren surely realized we did not have gasoline money to make the 50-mile round trip from Nashville to Gladeville twice every Sunday; we always spent the entire day there and were never without a luncheon invitation for the entire two years!

I took note that we ate more Sunday lunches with the Hunts than any other members. It was not until the end of our years there Mrs. Hunt revealed to me she had predetermined to prepare lunch and have it ready for us every Sunday if we were not invited elsewhere.

"Are these plates for Mr. Joe and Mis Wooby?" queried her young daughter after Joe and I had been their guests several times in succession, for it became her job to help her mother set the table each Sunday morning.

Mrs. Hunt did not "advertise" her good works but quietly confessed to me prior to our leaving Gladeville, "It was my way of helping our minister, since I was unable to contribute money for his schooling."

* * *

Joe taught the adult Bible class each Sunday morning and preached morning and evening sermons. We spent each Sunday afternoon visiting in members' homes, making calls to the sick, or in Bible study with someone. Occasionally we went out on a Saturday to take the teenagers on an outing. Also, periodically the Walker family hosted a Saturday church picnic in the large fenced area surrounding their old Victorian home. On those occasions, they invited us to spend the night. We slept on an ancient four-poster Victorian bed – a new experience for me – and were treated to a sumptuous Sunday-morning country breakfast.

The Walker family was a particularly large one, but they were hospitable Christians. They owned a farm in the community and made their living by truck farming and grew some of the finest and tastiest vegetables I have ever eaten. If they had produce left over after carrying a load to their Nashville market, they sometimes shared a bushel or two with us. They and one other family are the only brethren who ever offered us money when they knew we were especially pinched for cash. We accepted neither offer, but I shall carry to the grave with me the memory of their love and generosity.

Joe performed a wedding ceremony for one of the Walker daughters while he served as the church's minister. Both the bride and the groom were our seniors by several years. Following the wedding, the bride's parents served a wedding dinner in their home. This was the first wedding dinner to which Joe and I had been invited. On one side of their spacious house the inside walls of the rooms could be opened to form one huge, long room, to entertain large groups of guests. Tables were set up, end to end, across those open rooms to accommodate the 50 guests. They were overlaid with sparkling white linens and floral arrangements, perhaps from their garden; and a bountiful supply of home-cooked food was served.

OLD DIFFERENCES SURFACE

Joe has always been calm and coolheaded, and once I became inured to some awkward moments a few brethren caused me, I became quite a calm person, myself. I confess, however, in my older years, calmness sometimes eludes me.

Our time with the Glade brethren was generally completely pleasant in every way; however, one prickly situation arose during the summer between Joe's school years, when he was serving in Mississippi. We were told later that it was evidence of an old, festering conflict which existed before our coming there but of which we knew nothing. Thankfully, it was quickly quashed.

Some of the Glade men called a meeting and spoke openly of a plan to tell Joe, upon his return from Mississippi, he was no longer needed there, though all of them had agreed to release him for the summer to earn full-time pay, with the understanding he would return in the fall and be with them the following school year.

Other brethren reacted quickly to quash this bold plan.

Neither Joe nor I was aware of what was taking place until one of the brethren called me immediately following the meeting and informed me, concluding with the assurance Joe would not be dismissed – neither behind his back nor openly. The brethren's earlier promise to him would be honored. The brother told me to inform Joe of the situation but we were not to worry – not for one moment.

Nothing was said to Joe upon our return to Gladeville in the fall. He even received a weekly raise from $25 to $30! Nevertheless, the opposing brethren's idea didn't exactly die; they just developed a backup plan!

Later that year, when a visiting brother conducted a series of gospel meetings for the church, one evening following the regular worship, he was asked openly whether Joe should be dismissed owing to holding to a false doctrine. The wise man asked whether Joe had been preaching a false doctrine; the inquisitor was forced to answer in the negative or lie before the entire audience, all of whom were still sitting in their pews with bated breath.

After a moment's hesitation, he responded, "No," but added, "I'm sure he holds false views."

The guest minister quickly responded that no minister should be fired for holding a private view. He stated further that if Joe held a false view of anything, he was likely remaining silent until he could determine the truth about it before venturing to preach anything about it from the pulpit. That comment resolved the matter, and all was peaceful the remainder of our time there.

CLOSE TO HOME

On weekdays we left the apartment about the same time. Joe usually arrived home in the afternoon, however, before I did. I recall he once started our weekly laundry. He placed my red two-piece Sunday dress in the washing machine with our white clothes. The red dye leached until the dress was faded almost beyond recognition, and all the white clothes were dyed pink – sheets, undergarments, and all! Thus, ended Joe's laundering career!

Joe soon met two couples whom we knew from our days at FHC. They were sweethearts then, as were we, and now all of us were married. For most of the two years, we each took turns preparing Friday-evening meals for all three couples. Whenever it was my turn to cook, four of us had to sit on our bed, as we had only two chairs in our efficiency apartment in East Nashville. We also occasionally attended basketball games together or other functions on campus. We saw an old movie about the life of Martin Luther; and we heard the popular actor, Hal Holbrook, performing Mark Twain on stage. We were also privileged to see the Harlem Globetrotters entertain on the DLC basketball court.

After we moved near campus and had room for house guests, friends/relatives occasionally came to Nashville for the weekend to see the Grand Ole Opry, which had long since become a famous radio program. We provided lodging for them; in turn, they paid our way to see the "Opry" performed on stage. It was a pleasant diversion for us.

WE START A FAMILY

Even as a child I knew I wanted a family, and a few times I even dreamed of having blue-eyed, fair-skinned, blond-headed children! Prior to our marriage, Joe and I discussed that subject, and both agreed we wanted children. We both were happy when I became pregnant during Joe's senior year at DLC.

At that time, women did not flaunt their pregnancy during the early months or wear clothing intended to emphasize their bulging abdomens; nor were they seen in public as often as is common nowadays. Also, at that time, it was unusual for pregnant women to be permitted to remain in a secular job past seven months' pregnancy. Such was the case with me at Southern Bell.

One problem for me was that our budget was so tight; we had no money for maternity clothes. Angels stepped in, however. By the time I needed maternity clothes, I'd received a package from Mother, containing two ensembles she had lovingly sewn for me. One skirt was made of sturdy navy cotton with a lighter blue blouse that boasted a white collar and sleeve cuffs trimmed in white lace; the second skirt was of the same quality cotton, but brown in color, with a matching multicolored blouse. Though covered by the tops, both skirts had cutouts around the stomach area, allowing for expansion as the pregnancy progressed; and the waistband had adjustable ties on either side of the front opening. Those two became my Sunday clothes, and I wore them turnabout to worship throughout the remainder of my nine-months term.

In addition, I was delighted when a coworker who had saved an entire box full of maternity clothes from an earlier pregnancy offered to let me use them. Those became my wardrobe for work. I duly returned them to her when Southern Bell placed me on leave at the end of seven months' pregnancy. My supervisor gave me a full year's leave and begged me to promise to return to work at the year's end, saying there was a bright future for me with the Company; but I was determined to be a stay-at-home mother to my children, a decision I have never regretted, though it cost certain sacrifices.

Everyone in my work group presented me with a baby shower. From the "kitty" to which every employee contributed a quarter each payday, they lavished me with a high chair of excellent quality. (It was still in excellent condition after all three of our children had used it. Many years later, we gave it to one of Joe's employees when he and his wife were expecting a child.)

Homebound during the last two months, I saved the dresses Mother had earlier fashioned for me, Joe and I hoped to be blessed with additional children in the future. That sacrifice left me with nothing but some of Mother's old cotton dresses which she discarded when she lost so much weight. I took a brief walk almost daily and stopped twice each week to weigh on the penny scales which stood on the outside of the store nearest our apartment. What a sight I must have appeared to those whom I sometimes met on my walks!

The sisters of the Gladeville congregation honored us with a shower also, making sure that we had sufficient clothing and all other necessary articles to care initially for our new arrival.

The fee for my obstetrician's service, including all pre- and post-delivery visits was $150. We had no insurance, but we had the entire amount paid before the arrival of our child. We named our beautiful daughter Angelyn Gay, partially in honor of her Grandmother Pruett, whose name was Hettie Gay.

If memory serves me correctly, we paid nothing in addition for my four-day hospital stay. Perhaps another angel paid the hospital bill! I am sure I have been touched by angels in several instances in my life.

Wallace stood in for my husband, signing Joe's name on all paperwork when Baby Angelyn and I were dismissed from the hospital, for it was a

Sunday morning, and Joe was still filling the pulpit at Gladeville. The hospital staff asked Wallace multiple times if he were my husband. He explained faithfully each time he was asked, but his explanation never seemed to be understood or satisfy them. At length, he became no little frustrated and began to answer quite vocally, "Yes, I am her husband!" After a couple of his less-than-honest responses, the nurses apparently "understood," for there were no further questions!

Joe's parents let it be known they had "ordered" a grandson, but they had to wait some additional years before God granted their order. Joe and I were so thankful for all three children which God eventually gave us. I sincerely believe no mother has ever enjoyed rearing her children any more than I enjoyed rearing ours. Nor has any mother ever taken child rearing any more seriously than I.

FIRST SETTING IN ALABAMA (1957-58)

Prior to his graduation, Joe had been invited to become the minister for the Trinity, Alabama congregation, located a few miles outside Decatur, with the understanding he would preach for another nearby congregation, Piney Chapel, a heavy load even for a young man.

We were scheduled to move immediately following Joe's graduation in early June, for my due date was May 23. But as poet Robert Burns aptly stated, "The best laid plans go oft awry!"

The baby didn't arrive until June 12, 23 days after the date established by my obstetrician. It was another two weeks before the doctor gave me permission to travel, so Joe went ahead as planned, leaving Angel and me behind for a few weeks. Even then, my physician insisted I fly to Alabama.

We moved into the small but comfortable parsonage next door to the church house, owned by the brethren. We furnished it sparsely, and Joe settled into his work with little help from me; Angel was a sickly baby and required all my attention and energy.

One special blessing was the friendship which developed between Joe and an older, seasoned minister, Doyle Banta, who served a congregation in Decatur. The two of them paid weekly visits to a tuberculosis sanitorium a few miles outside Decatur. The older brother also offered us good advice on several occasions.

MEMORABLE FIRSTS
AT TRINITY

Once, Joe was asked to serve as substitute teacher for two weeks at Athens Bible School, a Christian school approximately 20 miles away. He agreed but came home every afternoon looking exhausted. Though he said little, it was obvious he was not enjoying the work. At the end of the two weeks, he came through the door saying he would not agree to be a substitute teacher ever again! He stuck by that resolve, but I never knew exactly why his experience was so disagreeable.

One Sunday morning, just before 9, a sister who was scheduled to prepare communion bread called and asked me to bake it, explaining her oven wasn't working properly. Morning services were at 10 and 11. Not only had I never made communion bread, I was busy trying to get the baby bathed and both of us ready to attend services. I informed the sister as much, along with some trepidation. Perhaps she didn't hear me, for she immediately began to tell me what a simple task it was to make unleavened bread. She named the simple ingredients required and also how to knead and bake it.

I was agitated and nervous, but I had no choice but to try my hand at it. Providence was with me; I didn't make it to the first service, but I had the bread, Angel, and myself ready and at the church house just before the latter service began. Since that time, I have accumulated various recipes for communion bread and have made vast amounts for some large congregations; but I've never forgotten how reluctantly I attempted preparing that first batch.

When Angel was just a few months old, I left her with a neighbor once, so one of the sisters of the congregation and I could visit a sick member in the hospital in Decatur. We planned to do our weekly grocery shopping afterwards. Neither of us knew the exact location of the hospital, so I turned down a side street a block away from it. When I realized I had taken a wrong turn, I used the nearest drive to turn around. Before I could finish my turn, a woman appeared at my window, holding a mop in her hand. I rolled down the window, thinking I would tell her my plight and ask if she could direct me to the hospital. Before I could speak one word, she brandished her mop in my face and told me, not once, but several times, I was breaking the law by using her driveway and she intended to call the police. I was shaking all over by the time she hesitated long enough to catch a breath.

Meantime, I found my voice long enough to say, "I apologize for using your driveway, ma'am, but if you will take your mop out of my face and leave me alone, I promise I will never come down this street again, much less enter your driveway!"

"You'd better not," was her reply, "or I'll have you arrested!"

I was still ashen and shaking with fear when the sister and I finished our errands and made our way back home. It was more than thrilling to see the sincere, sweet grin on my child's face when she was handed back to me.

FRIENDS AND NEIGHBORS

There was a young lady in the Trinity congregation, Carolyn Sims, who had attended FHC the same year Joe and I were there. She was then married to Dovell Haley, and the couple had a young son, Timothy, the same age as Angel. We became friends with them, and especially enjoyed sharing experiences about our little ones.

We agreed to have their combined first-birthday party at our house. Carolyn and I prepared each a cake for our children. After eating dinner, while the honorees sat in their high chairs, we presented each with a birthday cake, sang "Happy Birthday" to them, then distanced ourselves to observe their reactions.

Timothy took one look and immediately bent over and dug his entire little face into the cake, as though eager to consume the entire thing. Angel sat for a few minutes just staring at hers before she began to pick at it gently with her tiny right index finger, as if trying to discover what it was! (Don't tell me there is no difference between males and females!)

The elderly couple next door to us befriended us and often brought over a pan of homemade yeast rolls. That kind of hospitality will win friends anywhere! She once told me about an experience with one of her young grandsons, who followed her into the bathroom and was fascinated when he observed her remove her false teeth for cleaning.

He proceeded to ask her, "Grandma, can you remove your tongue too?"

Once, when she was away, her husband accepted our invitation to dinner one evening. He was thin and wiry and reminded us he had long since lost his appetite and could manage to get only a few bites down.

During his visit, he recalled how the worldwide influenza had struck his entire community during the winter of 1917-18, which had prostrated entire families and had led to the deaths of many. He managed to avoid the illness and aided every family. He took it upon himself to go from house to house throughout the community and chop wood for each family, place it on the front porch but never enter the house. I continue to regard him as an angel of mercy, akin to Florence Nightingale or Clara Barton.

ILLNESSES

Angel was a sickly child until she was past six years old. Perhaps it started when I was unable to nurse her after the first few weeks, for my body failed to produce milk, and no formula agreed with her. She vomited up most of it and continually had a sour breath, and a frequent elevated temperature, often accompanied by a rash.

Almost as soon as she finished one round of antibiotics, her symptoms recurred. The pediatrician finally told us one blessing was that she was building up immunities and would probably be a healthy adult. Adulthood has proven the doctor's prediction a correct one, but it was of little help at the time.

When Angel was about seven months, I miscarried my subsequent pregnancy. In my naïveté, I wasn't sure what was happening and didn't see a physician right away. When I finally consented to go, the doctor said I must be hospitalized for a few days for a D&C. I began to cry, telling him we had no money and no insurance – and for that reason I could not possibly enter the hospital.

That kindly Christian doctor said he would make all arrangements for me, and we could pay in installments afterward. I remained hospitalized three days, but we had the bill paid in full within three months, after which we managed to buy some kind of limited health insurance, trimming our slim budget even more.

Another difficulty arose during the winter of 1957-58, a 14-inch snowstorm. We were without electricity and water for one entire week. Joe manually lit the gas furnace, so each day we placed a wash tub filled with snow on the floor furnace and heated it in order to wash Angelyn's soiled diapers – no easy task for one with a queasy stomach like mine!

In the midst of making do, I developed an abscess in one of my wisdom teeth, which necessitated two trips to the dentist, a prescription, and more bills! Fortunately, the Lord was seeing after us, as always, for we had purchased a huge sack of potatoes, a jar of peanut butter, and plenty of crackers, largely on which we lived until our budget could recover from the additional bills.

In recalling these circumstances. I do not wish sympathy; I am simply relating many of our experiences, which are indelibly imprinted on my psyche. I confess, however, that we failed to develop the intimacy with the congregation we should have liked to do. No doubt, it was our fault. I, in particular, was absorbed with worry over our sick child, plus the fact that it was a constant struggle to keep all bills paid because her illness placed a greater financial burden on us. We paid all bills, nevertheless.

GORDON, GEORGIA
(1958-60)

After one year at Trinity, we were invited to move to Georgia, to work with the Hardy's Chapel congregation, located on State Highway 18, a few miles outside the town of Gordon. The location accommodated both Gordon and the community of Gray. I do not recall the salary offered, but it was some increase of pay, which we badly needed. God blessed our lives there in so many ways.

The town of Gordon served the local kaolin-mining industry. A broad and deep vein of kaolin (chalk) was discovered in that area during the early 1800s and mining operations had been in progress for 150 years. It was grayish in color when it came from the bowels of the earth; after refining, it was white and used in hundreds of items: chalk, medications, shoe polish, cleaners, to name a few.

During our time there, the mining remained in operation with three eight-hour shifts per day, seven days a week. With the exception of ministers and a few people who owned businesses in town, the breadwinner of every family worked in the mine, and we were told there was sufficient chalk in the broad kaolin vein to keep operations active for at least 150 additional years.

Except for the highest echelon of company officials, shifts of all the employees rotated each week, so each three weeks' time every employee had worked a different shift and everyone made good wages. Their schedule allowed the men more than enough time to care for family affairs. Golfing was their recreation of choice. Joe was quickly invited to join some of the brethren in this sport weekly for the entire time we lived in Gordon.

* * *

Everyone we met there received us with a warm welcome and friendliness. From the moment we arrived, we fell in love with the easygoing, kind people of the congregation of approximately 125 members, others as well; all reciprocated that love. Never before (nor since) have we felt more kinship and love in any place we have lived. Angel soon had two favorite playmates, Pam and Marsha, whose parents, Frank and Patty Hawthorne, became our best friends.

There was perfect harmony within the congregation. The church had elders, good shepherds who watched for the souls of all those whom they served, as they that "must give an account" to God, and the congregation thrived. In addition, the city fathers and civic leaders always invited us to attend any special occasions they hosted and asked Joe to offer the prayers.

Joe has never asked for a specific amount of money from any congregation, nor has he ever asked for a raise. He has accepted, without question, whatever the brethren offered. I'm sure one of the members of the church realized we could use some extra income, for he came unexpectedly to our house one day with an offer for me.

"Ruby, my brother-in-law is county superintendent of Wilkinson County Public Schools and is in need of another teacher. Get ready. I'll take you to see him, and you can begin teaching in our school system if you wish."

I was holding our Angel at the time. I looked down at her and said, "I appreciate your offer to help me, and God knows we could use the money; but I cannot leave my baby."

* * *

Joe and I were so pleased and thankful to God for the opportunity to assist in forming two new congregations in Georgia during our years in Gordon. The first one was at Milledgeville, the state's first capital. A few Christians had already begun meeting in one brother's house when we moved to

Gordon, and we quickly became involved in building up that work. Within two years, the church had its own building and was prospering.

The Hardy's Chapel congregation was directly responsible for starting a new congregation in Forsythe, Georgia. We rented what had been an old service station, and several members of Hardy's Chapel helped us renovate it and convert it into a temporary dwelling for church services. Joe conducted the first gospel meeting there as soon as it was in suitable condition.

I shall always remember one day in particular when several of us worked at Forsythe an entire long hot day, but no one had brought food. We worked like Trojans, and everyone grew famished. We pooled what money we had and sent someone to the nearest rural grocery store. That dear brother returned with a couple of loaves of bread, a jar of mayonnaise, a can of sliced pineapple, and a few tomatoes. Never have I tasted a more delicious lunch than we shared in common that day.

Another example of the brethren's love and generosity manifested itself when Joe and I were in need of a loan to trade vehicles. A brother insisted on accompanying us to the bank and being a co-signer of the loan but revealed no reason for his action.

We assured him it was not necessary, for we felt capable of handling our own financial affairs. We'd paid every cent of Joe's college expenses on our own; in fact, we had lived independently ever since our marriage.

Still, the brother insisted on going! He signed the note, which puzzled us greatly. Much later we learned that a minister who had served the congregation in the past had left the area without paying all his debts. Then we understood our brother wished to protect the bank's investment in us as well as the church's reputation. I'm sure he was pleased never to be held responsible for the money.

* * *

One afternoon, when Joe and I attended a parade downtown, crowded with people on a rather warm summer day, a young man standing behind me tapped me on the shoulder.

When I turned to him, he asked, "Do you know where a fellow can buy a beer around here? I'm dying with thirst for a beer!"

My inquirer drew an instant conclusion when I responded with, "Sorry, no, I don't."

"Oh, you're new around here, too, ain't you?"

As I recall, I just grinned but made no further reply.

* * *

Perhaps it was because I helped Mother when I was young that sewing just seemed to come naturally for me. In addition to mending Joe's and my underclothing and socks, I sewed the first dresses Angel had, completely by hand, for we owned no sewing machine until Mother's first visit to Gordon, when she offered a loan sufficient for me to purchase a machine. I accepted and we chose a new Singer machine. I repaid Mother every cent of the loan in $10 monthly installments.

When one of the sisters in the congregation learned I had a new sewing machine, she invited me to join her in registering for sewing classes in Macon, 18 miles away. Each session lasted six weeks, with one full day of instruction each week. At the end of each term, every student had completed one outfit. The instructor was outstanding, and I have always been delighted that I took advantage of her ability, for I greatly improved my sewing skills under her direction and since then have sewn hundreds of ensembles for the family and gifts for others.

A STARR DESCENDS

Another special blessing was the birth of our second child, a daughter whom we named Melanie Starr. She was born in the hospital at Macon, weighing in at almost 10 pounds, the largest infant in the maternity ward at the time. Unlike Angel, Starr was a contented and healthy baby. She gained weight quickly and consistently and turned over in her crib the day she became two months old!

Frank and Patty were delighted to care for Angel the four days I was hospitalized. Just short of her third birthday when her little sister was born, Angel had obviously already been taught against smoking, for when our friends brought her home, Frank related to me that Angel had marched into his bedroom one evening and discovered him smoking a cigarette. She placed her hands on her hips and announced, "Now, Mista Fwank, you know you shudn't smoke!"

Frank teasingly accused me of putting her up to that.

A few days later Angel announced to me, "Mama, you can go to the hospital any time you want to and get another baby. Mista Fwank and Miss Patty will take care of me!"

PREPARATION FOR
FOREIGN WORK

Minister Connie Adams conducted a gospel meeting at Hardy's Chapel in early 1959. He had spent a few years as a missionary in Norway; and during his time among us, he began to encourage us to do the same. Perhaps we were too young and inexperienced to count the cost, but we made the difficult decision to go there, and we soon set about making plans to leave Gordon the following year, but not before we flew to Medicine Hat, Alberta, Canada for a two-week gospel meeting hosted by Joe's sister and brother-in-law, Joe and Roemayne Corley, who were living there at the time.

Once we returned from Canada, we began serious planning. Though the Hardy's Chapel brethren wanted us to remain with their congregation, they supported us wholeheartedly in our new endeavor and granted us all the time necessary for preparations. We ordered an excellent set of records and books on the Norwegian language and spent time each day studying it. Joe spent a great deal of time traveling to various congregations, enlisting financial support from those who wished to sponsor us. Expecting our second child, I remained at home with Angel, allowing me more time to study the language. Still, both of us were able to converse in the language sufficiently to communicate to some degree with the crew and guests aboard the *Oslo Fjord* when we sailed for Bergen, Norway, in August of the following year.

We disposed of our few possessions (except a few special mementos and our wedding gifts of crystal and china, which we stored at Mom and

Pop Pruett's). Then we bade a tearful goodbye to our Gordon friends and brethren before Frank and Patty drove us to Atlanta for the nine-day journey to a foreign land.

We attended a worship service with some brethren in New York City and spent the night with them. Our host brother drove us to the pier, where we boarded the *Oslo Fjord* the following morning. The 10-mile distance required almost two hours in the New York traffic.

I prepared a supply of bottles of formula for Starr before we left New York, but I was so tense and distracted I left them in the refrigerator where we had spent the night. Another American came to my rescue once we were aboard ship, and one of the nurses onboard quickly appeared with a new supply of both bottles and milk for the entire voyage.

Disposable diapers were just then becoming popular, but it never occurred to me to be so extravagant as to buy them – not even for crossing the ocean with a four-months-old baby in tow! Hence, a part of my daily routine was washing Starr's soiled diapers, by hand (usually 14 daily) in the huge laundry room.

One day, a Norwegian woman was ironing when I went into the laundry. When she had finished, she came over to where I was washing diapers and asked, "Vil De bruke strykkejern?" (Would you like to use the iron now?)

I was unfamiliar with the word for iron, so I responded, "Jeg forstar ikke," (I don't understand.).

She continued to repeat the question; each time I answered the same way. After I had repeated the same answer four times, she blurted out with obvious irritation, "De forstar ingenting!" Then she quickly took her leave of me.

Those words I understood; they meant I understood nothing! I was a bit humiliated!

Otherwise, all went fairly smoothly during the eight days at sea. The housekeeper, or "Tante," appeared at the door of our stateroom three times daily, apparently eager to care for Starr and tidy the room while we went for meals. Each time we returned, Tante was usually still humming a tune to Starr, who seemed always perfectly content. Once upon our return, Starr was grasping a tiny American flag in one hand and a tiny Norwegian one in the other. I do not recall how much we tipped Tante at journey's end, but I have often thought she deserved several times that amount!

NORWEGIAN YEARS (1960-64)

When we arrived in Bergen after eight days at sea, some of the Christians there met and greeted us with outspread arms. We were soon ensconced in our apartment.

Friends and relatives occasionally mailed packages containing goodies that were not available there, but there was no means of instant communication; and intercontinental telephone service was extremely costly, so we could only make contact with loved ones back home via mail. Only God knows how homesick I became at times! I would think of Mother's yeast rolls and homemade sausage and burst into tears. However, after weeping for a while, I recovered sufficiently to carry on my normal routine.

Norway is a small democratic socialist country, which means the government exercises control of education, health, religion, transportation, and more. Before Catholicism gained sway, Norway was a pagan nation. Catholicism was replaced by Lutheranism as the State religion, and we were informed that 97% of the Norwegians people claimed membership in that church. There were many exquisite edifices in which they took great pride; but when we visited their worship, the number of congregants didn't show evidence of that figure.

Even though the country boasted freedom of religion, our work was difficult and slow. History proves that no country steeped for centuries in one religion would release its hold on its citizens with no hesitation. A few times we were told to return home. When that happened, we never failed to remind them their country practices freedom of religion, giving us the right to be there, since we met their requirements for entry into their country.

CULTURAL DIFFERENCES

Shortly after our arrival in the country, we were confronted with the fact that small children do not customarily attend adult worship, for they cause distraction. It was pointed out to us only after we had been bringing our young Starr for several weeks. She was a quiet, contented baby, but it is true that children can and do sometimes disturb worship, causing distraction.

We were pained that we had not been informed of the problem earlier but did not know exactly what to do. We had met only a few Norwegians at the time, and I refused to leave Starr with someone whom we did not know or who came to us without recommendation. We immediately wrote a dear Christian elder, whom I loved and admired, but we never received a response.

We had occasion to see that brother while we were back in the States after serving two years. I asked whether he had received our letter.

"Yes, was his answer.

I said, "I never heard from you."

He told me he had discussed our problem with the church's minister, who took the letter and promised to respond to it. I was disappointed to hear his answer but glad to know it was not my respected friend who had failed me.

Both Joe and I were disappointed we had not learned sooner about something that affected us so directly, for we did not wish to offend the country's custom, so we agreed on a compromise: We would continue to bring Starr to the day services – the young people loved seeing her and holding her – and leave her home in the evening. We were obliged to hire a teenager to care for her two or more evenings a week. She seemed fond of Starr and always enjoyed our snacks but was careless about cleaning up. Once we came home to discover a knife smeared with peanut butter lying on the bed, a few smears on the bedspread, in addition.

CLOTHING, FOOD,
AND LANGUAGE

We began dressing like the Norwegians and continued to study their rhythmic language. Soon we spoke only Norwegian, even in the home, and the Norwegians began to think of us as one of them. Angel, in her fourth year when we arrived, was the only one who struggled a few months. She didn't understand the language in her new environment, so she would not even converse with us in English but remained silent. Concerned, we sought permission to enroll her in kindergarten. She quickly adjusted and in short time became so fluent she asked us not to speak in "that language" she no longer understood – meaning English. Conversely, Starr's first words were, quite naturally, spoken in Norwegian, for she was only four months old when we arrived in Norway.

Angel and Starr made friends easily with the Norwegian children, and I soon made them each an everyday "bunad" (costume), and a dressy one to be worn only on special occasions.

Each district of Norway has its own costume design; I chose the Hardanger pattern for both styles. Our granddaughters have inherited those dress costumes, and I hope to see them on my great granddaughters someday.

For dinner, Norwegians usually eat fish five days a week, gruel on Saturday and flesh (beef or pork), on Sundays. Fishing boats come ashore each day with their fresh catch. Norwegians do everything with fish that Americans do with ground beef (i.e., they prepare fish cakes, fish balls, and fish loaf), but their standard meal is boiled fish. Angel, in particular, relished it all, but Joe and I missed our southern-fried chicken! When we learned of a specialty store in downtown Bergen that imported small fryers from England, we hastened to buy a couple and fried them for our Sunday dinner.

Both Angel and Starr "licked the bones," after which Angel burst forth in her childish Norwegian, "Mama, I do not know what kind of meat this is, but it is so-o-o-o-o good!"

Maybe Southern love of fried chicken can be inherited!

MISSION WORK

Our work was divided between Stavanger and Bergen. We began work in Bergen, followed by a stint in Stavanger, then back to Bergen when the congregation purchased the entire second floor of a building on Nattlandsvei, and we lived in the apartment section of that floor the remainder of our stay.

Joe and the other missionaries with whom we worked, at least a portion of our stay there, worked diligently to translate English pamphlets and tracts into Norwegian, with the help of a young Norwegian convert. They distributed them among the people, arranged private Bible studies as opportunity afforded itself, and placed ads in newspapers. Both men and women taught the children's classes and came to love all the young people dearly. Their parents allowed them to come to classes and to our apartment for parties, but they were too deeply entrenched in their country's customs to allow their young freely to become "one of us."

We reached out in other ways, visiting nursing homes and bringing food to the ill. One lady in a nursing home I remember distinctly, for she had a favorite hymn, "Nearer, Still Nearer," which she asked us to sing every time we came to visit her. As soon as she recognized us, she would immediately begin to hum it. Even today, every time we sing that song in worship, I think of her and sometimes just can't help singing a portion of the words in Norwegian. Another popularly requested song was, "Nothing but the Blood of Jesus."

We once received a call from an elderly Norwegian woman who requested a visit. When we arrived, she told us her story. She had been reading her Bible for many years and seeking Christ's church. She added that when she read the Acts of the Apostles and other scriptures, she understood baptism was a literal burial in water, not just a sprinkling or pouring on the candidate. She had many times asked her priest to administer that rite for her and completely submerge her in water, but he had steadfastly refused, thinking it unnecessary, and dismissed her as an eccentric. She refused to yield until he did indeed immerse her, just to free himself of her importunity.

She added she was delighted to see Christ's church advertised in the paper. She was never able to attend services but gave of her means to the Lord and supported the church's work to her dying day. It is likely rare that this sort of conversion happens, but her story proves anyone can study God's word independently and possibly reach the same conclusion.

One afternoon a teenager Joe had been teaching ran into our apartment after school and excitedly told Joe the priest had taught his class that day the same thing Joe had taught – that instrumental music was not introduced into the church until centuries after the church came into existence. (I have wondered if the reason for this is that Christians were persecuted and killed during the early years of this "new religion" and were forced to worship quietly in hiding or flee for their life, which would surely have made the logistics of using musical instruments in worship a difficult endeavor.)

We once received an Italian minister into our home for an extended period of time to conduct special services for the church. He had been converted from a high position in the Catholic Church in Rome and revealed many things to us concerning his past. One superior counseled him, "Do not leave us, or you will surely marry and have a family."

"But, Father, isn't that better than priests who break their vows of celibacy?"

The brother also revealed to us that when some of the young Christian men learn God's grace covers sins, no matter how great or how many, they conclude it is safe to commit as many sins as they wish – and in this way receive more grace while satisfying any/all fleshly desires.

A Visit Home

At the end of two years, we were permitted to return home for a few weeks so Joe could report on our work to those who had contributed toward our support. I stayed with Mother as often and for as long as I could. That summer she was living with her eldest sister, who seemed disinclined to welcome my two small daughters and me. Otherwise, I stayed with Joe's parents and briefly with other relatives.

In addition, the girls and I traveled with Joe occasionally, if specifically invited by the host church/family. It was difficult leaving family, but good to have my family intact again when we took our second ocean voyage to Norway at the end of three months.

During that Atlantic crossing, a terrific storm arose, lasting three days. Not only did all the passengers become deathly seasick, but the ship's crew also. What a relief when the storm passed!

Crossing the Atlantic from New York City to Norway was an 8-day voyage. The bursar approached Joe and asked if he were willing to conduct Sunday-morning worship aboard ship.

"I'd be happy to do so, Sir, but we sing hymns a cappella only in our worship," replied Joe.

"No problem," said the bursar.

When we entered the salon where worship was to be conducted, a band was playing for many of the passengers gathered there. At exactly 10 a.m. the music stopped, and Joe's audience was in place! He conducted the worship the same as he would in any other setting. We were happy for such a special opportunity to meet and speak to some of the passengers whom we would never have had occasion to do otherwise.

HEALTH ISSUES

The Norwegian government permitted us to purchase government-run health insurance, at the same premium rate the Norwegians paid. It became a great blessing, as we had several occasions to use it.

Angel's tonsils and adenoids were constantly infected, such that her pillow began to be stained with blood each night. The condition affected her ears, and she became almost completely deaf. Eventually the doctor said she needed surgery. I was told parents could not stay with their children in the hospital but must leave the premises as soon as a child was admitted, so I innocently asked the doctor whether we could rent a room adjoining Angel's, for I did not wish to leave her in the hands of strangers at such a time.

He stared at me as if in total disbelief. "If you insist on that, I will not perform surgery on your child." With that, he dismissed us.

Angel's illness persisted, so we returned to the physician, saying, "Our child must have help, and we will follow any rules you impose."

We brought Angel to the hospital on the appointed day, where she remained for 14 days, some of the longest days of my life.

"You may leave now." Said the nurse to us as she handed us Angel's clothes within a few minutes of our arrival.

"May we be with her on the on the day of her surgery?" I asked.

"You may come and sit in the lobby during the time of her surgery if you wish, but you will not be permitted to see her," were the discouraging words the nurse uttered.

We complied, as painful as it was for us and surely for Angel, too. On the day of the surgery, we sat in the lobby, quietly praying all the while, and wishing with all our heart we could be with her to comfort her.

Afterward, the surgeon came to us and said Angel had survived the surgery, followed with the same words we had heard earlier, "You may leave now."

Only one time during that long two weeks did we receive permission to drive by and wave to our precious little girl while a nurse held her up to the window momentarily.

I learned after Angel was dismissed how traumatic her experience had been. She was in a ward with 16 other children and spanked by her nurse for refusing to allow the nurse to undress her. Angel said each time the nurse pulled her panties down, she pulled them up again, asking all the while for her mama and papa. After the battle ensued back and forth several times, the nurse spanked Angel until she yielded.

Angel was so traumatized during those two long weeks in the hospital that a long time afterward, every time she saw someone wearing a white jacket or hospital scrubs, she would run to us and cling, saying, "Mama and Papa, let's go home now!" She has never forgotten her fright and the way she was treated because of it. However, she did heal physically, and her hearing eventually returned to normal.

Joe was plagued with gallstones intermittently. Sometimes he was in such pain he would kneel in the floor in a praying position and literally cry. He was misdiagnosed a few times, but eventually a doctor determined it was gallstones and scheduled surgery – shortly after the birth of our third child.

Following his surgery, Joe remained in the ward with 15 other men for two weeks. The mother of one of Angel's friends volunteered to care for our infant son a few hours each afternoon of Joe's stay, allowing me to take a bus to the hospital to visit Joe. What a wonderful, loving thing to do! I have never forgotten her kindness.

Joe told me later the man in the bed next to him asked one day just after I left from one of my daily visits, "What district does your wife come from?' – he had detected a slight difference in my pronunciation of some Norwegian words.

Joe responded, "My wife is an American, and so am I."

The man said he could hardly believe his ears, for he thought both of us were natives! We were always happy to tell anyone we were Americans, but we considered the man's inquiry a compliment to our command of the Norwegian language.

JOE'S SPECIAL VACATION

During our third summer in Norway, Joe and the grandson of the lady who was our children's adopted grandmother (Bestemor), decided to take a camping trip through several European countries. They traveled through Denmark, Belgium, East and West Germany, and France. Joe made many slides of the wall dividing East Berlin from West Berlin and, years later, showed them to Tony's second-grade class. Joe still talks about the congested traffic in Paris and how no one paid heed to the policemen directing it.

At the time of their trip, I was pregnant and unable to travel with them. While they were away, I contracted pneumonia. With proper attention and having complete bed rest for several days, per our physician's demand, I soon recovered. My friend Kristi Augestad lived nearby and helped with the girls while I was confined to bed.

A SON AT LAST

It would have been totally uncommon, perhaps impossible, during our younger years for parents to know their child's sex prior to birth. We were happy to think of another addition to our family – I've always liked odd numbers! We both hoped for a son, but we'd agreed with this pregnancy it truly didn't matter, for a son could not be sweeter or finer than our two daughters. Still, Joe's parents continued to insist, yea, demand, we have a son each time I gave birth.

I saw a pediatrician regularly during the latter months of my pregnancy. Whether the custom continues to this day I know not, but midwives delivered babies, even in Norwegian hospitals, during the 1960s. A doctor's service was requested only when there was a serious birthing problem. Nor were expectant mothers permitted to enter the hospital until contractions were five minutes apart, and no one – not even the child's father – could remain at the hospital during labor, visit the mother or even see the newborn during her recovery in the hospital. My length of stay was four days. Not only that, but no one called Joe when Anthony Yates "Tony" Pruett arrived between 5 and 6 on the morning of November 28, 1963, even though I asked several times whether my husband had been notified. He first learned the good news that God had given us a son at last when he called the hospital at 9 a.m., four hours past the time of the baby's birth.

Joe arranged to bring Angel and Starr by the hospital on Saturday afternoon. He parked our Volkswagen Beetle on the street outside my room, and I spoke with them briefly through my window. Each was wearing her blouse backward; their braids were undone and their long hair blew loosely across their faces.

"Who dressed you and combed your hair?" I wondered aloud. "Papa tried," was Angel's quick response.

I realized Papa had done his best and said no more on the subject; but I still have the mental image of both girls' appearance and was delighted to be discharged on Sunday to be reunited with my family, and to present the newest member of our family to his older sisters.

I was particularly blessed with my faithful friend, Kristi, whose husband was an officer on a freighter which delivered supplies in ports all over the world. Kristi was permitted to travel with him some but was often home with their one son for extended periods of time. She willingly agreed to help me daily for two weeks after the baby's arrival.

She laundered clothing, kept the house clean, and prepared a delicious middag (dinner) for us each day throughout both weeks while I cared for our newborn. All our family loved her dearly.

After our return to America, Kristi and I corresponded in Norwegian, as she knew no English, and exchanged gifts until her death in 1988. Her memory will forever remain close to my heart as one of God's earthly angels who has touched my life.

RECREATION

During the winter months, snow blankets the entire country, and all inland roads are closed. Skiing is the popular and respected sport of all the Norwegians. I have more than once seen a city bus stop and wait patiently to allow a youngster to ski across the street!

Joe and Angel quickly learned to ski. I tried a time or two, but my old knee injury flared up, causing me great pain, so I gave up the idea quickly. As soon as Starr could walk, one of the brethren would fasten her on top of his skis and take her skiing, along with Joe and Angel.

Many Norwegians owned cottages in the country, which were covered with snow during the winter. They spent summer vacations there during those few, but long sunlit days, soaking up as much sun as possible. One summer, we were able to rent a lakeside cottage for a few days. We had to paddle a small boat about a quarter mile to reach it. We traveled by boat to the rural milk and bread station for those supplies, carrying our milk pail along. It was quite a pleasureful experience for our entire family.

The other activity most Norwegians enjoy is hiking/mountain climbing. On long summer days, I have seen older women taking walks as late as 11 p.m. Norway is truly the Land of the Midnight Sun.

Blueberries grow plentifully along the Norwegian mountainsides. When they were in season, it was delightful recreation for our family to find a safe place to pick a bucketful. Then we hurried home to make blueberry pancakes, a delicious treat! Our last fall there, we went picking not long before Tony was born. I recall clinging gingerly to tree branches as we climbed up the mountainside to reach the fruit.

Edward Grieg is Norway's most famous musician. An annual concert of his music is performed in his home. Joe and I were privileged to attend one of the concerts – and afterward to view the Griegs' burial place, a hewn-out rock facing a fjord of the North Sea at the back of his house. It made me think of Jesus' burial site provided by Joseph of Arimathea.

Also, we were once privileged to hear a relative of "God's Eager Fool," Albert Schweitzer, speak in Bergen about his life's work among disease-ridden natives, whose mission post was located at Lambarene in French Equatorial Africa.

TROUBLE IN THE CAMP

Our family adjusted well to living in Norway. Joe and I worked mainly with youngsters and teenagers and sustained a good relationship with them, which we trust has born much fruit in later years. We met many people, once we learned the proper way to be introduced. As native Southerners, our nature was friendly; whereas the more reserved Norwegians require a more formal means of introduction. Also, both Angel and Starr were "adopted" by an older neighbor, who became their Bestemor, at her request. She even crocheted warm Norwegian ensembles for their dolls, so they would be comfortable during the long, cold Norwegian winters!

Two new American families joined us in our third year of work, during the decades when great controversy existed in the brotherhood over how missionaries were to be supported (among other issues) and whether fellowship should be extended to brethren who differed on these issues - first century Christians were not immune to controversy. We had not introduced these problems to the Norwegians; nor did we think it wise to do so. We focused on teaching God's plan of salvation and the Bible recipe for living a godly life. We worked in concert with the Christians and their ministers in Oslo and other parts of the country.

Though we did our best to assist the new missionaries in adjusting to their new setting by giving them opportunity to grow in the language and the work in general, they soon disagreed with us for our "liberal" views, i.e., working with brethren with whom they disagreed; nor did they appreciate the fact that our worship differed slightly from the typical worship in America. No explanation seemed to satisfy them.

Consequently, these ministers were soon hinting we should return home, assuring us they were quite capable of handling the work alone. We became heart sick, for we were already praying about and contemplating spending our lives in Norway. We also wondered how leaving two unseasoned missionary families in the country might affect the work there. After much anguish, it seemed our staying there was not to be; we reluctantly returned to the States at the end of our fourth year. That unfortunate experience left both of us scarred. Still, it strengthened me, for it taught me a Christian may have problems from without and from within his sphere of work, but one must continue to be faithful to the Lord with no bitterness of heart (Joseph and the apostle Paul are perfect biblical examples of how to endure all kinds of suffering.)

We arranged to buy another Volkswagen Beetle before we left, for Joe did research and discovered he could buy the car in Germany and pay shipping to New York for more than $200 less than a new one would cost in the United States.

> For the last leg of our return trip, Joe decided he and Angel should travel from New York City in the new Volkswagen and Starr, Tony and I should fly to Memphis, where relatives would meet us.

Joe and Angel were already on their way before it was time to board our flight. I had difficulty holding Tony on my left arm and Starr's left hand in my right one, plus my purse and a carry-on bag strapped to my left shoulder. God sent me help, for a gentleman raced up to me before I entered the airplane and insisted on helping me. Fortunately, he was flying to Memphis also and insisted on staying with me, carrying my bag and clasping Starr's hand, until we were safely inside the terminal and in the arms of our relatives. I never knew who he was, but he was a great blessing, and I have often tried to repay such random kindness by aiding others who need assistance I could render.

On the flight, Starr sat beside a lady who tried to engage her in conversation by asking where she was going. Neither Angel nor Starr understood English for some months after our return, because they had heard only Norwegian for four years. I explained to Starr in Norwegian that the lady asked her where she was going.

Starr quickly responded, "Amerika," with a pronounced Norwegian inflection.

The lady gave me a puzzled look.

I explained our family had lived overseas virtually all of Starr's life, and as far as she knew, we were not in America until we arrived at our destination in the South!

Relatives were there to welcome us home, and we visited with them a few days before traveling to Alabama to serve the Skyline Drive congregation in the Corner community in the northwest section of Jefferson County.

Before leaving Obion, Joe had the pleasure of performing the wedding ceremony for my dear niece, Julia "Judy" Inman, and her groom, Charles "Butch" Grisham, at the Obion Church of Christ. I had not only pulled her many miles in her little red wagon when she was a baby, but baby sat her many a time during her pre-school days.

* * *

I missed Mother sorely during our years in Norway, and I determined our children should spend time with her and get to know her, now that we were back. I also decided I would never fail to spend Mother's birthday with her. I remained true to both commitments. My children still recall some pleasant visits with her, and there were 27 birthday celebrations before her decease.

Each year I did my best to have our entire family gathered for the celebration. I always carried Mother a huge birthday cake, in addition to other food. On one such trip. I stopped for gasoline at a service station in Mississippi. I had her huge cake on the back seat, in clear view through the back windows. As my tank was being filled, two disheveled, wobbling men appeared and walked around the car. Both appeared to have drunk too much.

One peeped through the window and exclaimed, "I see a birthday cake in this car," capturing the other's attention.

At that comment, both men peered inside.

"It says, 'Happy Birthday, Mama Yates.' Wonder who that is," the first one said. "Oh, how I wish I could have a piece that cake!"

All the while, I was sitting at the wheel, and I heard every word. Sympathy tempted me to offer each one a piece, but my saner side indicated it might not be the best idea, so I squelched my impulse.

* * *

Joe and I permitted our children to visit their Pruett grandparents as often as they were invited, but those visits were infrequent. Mom and Pop Pruett hosted their other grandchildren for long visits every summer. Perhaps the addition of our three would have been too burdensome.

BACK TO ALABAMA
(1964-99)

On leaving Norway, we had no immediate plans for our future, but depended on the Lord to guide us. Joe's sister and brother-in-law, Joe and Roemayne Corley, were currently serving the Skyline Drive church but were making plans to return to Alberta, Canada, where they had previously worked. They knew we were returning to the States in August 1964, and recommended us to the Skyline Drive brethren, who invited us to work there. They provided no parsonage, but the brethren were willing to co-sign notes in order for us to buy the Corleys' house next door to the church.

We had three children, and our only possessions were a new Volkswagen and $200 cash, plus the few salvageable items we had stored. We accepted their offer with grateful hearts and moved there in time for Angel to begin the first grade at Corner School.

God again supplied every need! On our first Sunday at Skyline, we met Jay and Fay Mikell and their sons, Andy and Tim. Jay worked for Tennessee Coal and Iron (TCI) in Birmingham and owned a furniture store in Sumiton. He and Fay hastened an offer for us to buy furniture at the wholesale company in Birmingham from which they purchased inventory. Jay insisted we could charge each item to the store and repay him as we had the means.

We were soon outfitted sufficiently to keep house once again and paid the debt completely in due time.

The greater blessing was that we were soon fast friends with Jay and Fay; they became Uncle Jay and Aunt Fay to our children. We often ate meals in each other's home and played cards afterward. Because Tony was always excited to see them come through our door and met them each time with several seconds of unintelligible chatter, they dubbed him their "welcoming committee!"

Fay and I attended a Liberace concert together in Birmingham. He was covered from head to toe in diamonds and flaunted them all. What a talented musician and showman he was!

Though Andy and Tim were older than our daughters, they played well together.

If they ever became a bit rowdy, Jay would say, "Ruby, why don't you spank Angel and Starr, so my boys could get the idea they must behave?"

We remained friends long after we moved away; and, years later, Joe performed the wedding ceremony for Andy and his beautiful young bride. Our last visit was only two weeks prior to Fay's death, and Jay's followed soon afterward.

FURTHER ADJUSTMENTS

After living in a bustling foreign city for four years, moving to a rural Southern community demanded some adjustments of everyone in the family except Tony, who was still too young to speak.

Joe found himself using Norwegian expressions in the pulpit for some time, which made the brethren look askance.

Angel's teacher did not understand why Angel knew none of the patriotic songs they sang in school. Nor was Angel aware of all the holidays Americans celebrate. Our first Halloween home, she had no doubt heard her classmates talk about what fun they would have that evening, collecting candy; when she exited the school bus that afternoon, she rushed into the house as though she could hardly wait to ask, "Mama, when are we going trigger treating?"

And one day near Christmas, she skipped around the den several times, repeating, "Mr. Santa Claus, Brother Santa Claus," as though trying to determine how to address Santa. We had taught our children to address men as Brother or Mister, so she assumed Santa should be respectfully addressed with one of those titles too.

Starr's main problem at first was the fact she could not have a "brun ost skive" (brown cheese sandwich) for lunch every day. It was a deliciously creamy, smooth, light-brown cheese eaten on an open-face slice of buttered bread – what all Norwegian children ate daily and had been Starr's choice for lunch ever since she began to talk.

I did my best to explain American children eat other kinds of cheese sandwiches and we had no brown cheese. She did not understand and refused to eat much of anything when I could not produce a brun ost skive for her. My heart ached for her, for it became noticeable that she was losing weight. Just when I was at wits' end and consulting with a local doctor, she began to eat and gradually adjusted to substituting yellow cheese or peanut butter sandwiches for the brown cheese ones.

After that, her adjustment went quite well, and she attended kindergarten in Warrior the following summer at age five. Her teachers told us she was ready to enter first grade.

Dealing with Angel and Starr's transition from one country and its language to another country and language was stressful for me. But nature itself became my personal stress reliever in our new setting. Viewing the dogwood trees that bloomed in great profusion the following spring – as they do every year – healed me. That first spring in Corner, I could hardly wait to take a bicycle ride down the long, level stretch of road in front of our house, and observe such natural beauty. My appreciation and awe of God's gift of those magnificent trees completed my transition. I fell in love with Alabama that spring, and that love remains in my heart.

Many years later, when I began taking oil-painting lessons from Helen Holladay, I purchased a painting of a dogwood tree in full bloom from her, in memory of that first spring in Corner, Alabama, when their beauty had inspired me, as Helen's art work did. I have subsequently painted two paintings of branches filled with dogwood blossoms.

FINANCES VERSUS RESPONSIBILITIES

Our income was meager, considering the cost of living for a family of five. The children seemed to understand our money was scarce. One day we were in Warrior, shopping with our friends, Fay and Jay. Noon arrived, so Jay and Fay suggested we have lunch at one of the little restaurants in town. Before Joe or I could respond, Starr spoke up, "Let's don't eat there. It will cost too much money!"

A little embarrassing but true. The brethren eventually permitted Joe to supplement his income with secular work.

A few years later, Tony came running into the house one day with some strong discarded cord he had found and which he wound around a small stick he picked up.

He handed it to me. "Here, Mama, I found some good string in the yard and saved it for you, for I knew we could use it!"

The children never complained, just accepted our circumstances. And God being my witness, as parents, both Joe and I tried to make the home life for them full of love and happiness, along with discipline and teaching the way of the Lord, both by word and example. We saw that they were able to participate in all their school and church activities, and others as well, as they grew up. Regardless of the means of any family, I firmly believe it is a good lesson for children to be taught to have an appreciation of finances and to be thrifty, not stingy, and to share their blessings with others as they have opportunity.

A minister's work is virtually the same whether at home or abroad. We taught private Bible studies. We not only visited the sick, but we visited in the home of every member, and hosted an annual picnic for the congregation. We continued doing these things until Joe's retirement. I taught children's Bible classes while Joe always taught adult classes. The congregation grew, as was the case in every church we served.

Invariably, some unusual/memorable, even unique incidents occurred wherever we lived. I recall vividly a wedding Joe performed at Corner. The young bride fainted right after the ceremony ended and was unable to attend the wedding reception.

Also, one private Bible study with an older gentleman resulted in a belated conversion. Years later, when the man was a patient in a Birmingham hospital, he called Joe, saying he had repented of his sins and was ready to confess his belief in Christ, and wished to be baptized as soon as possible.

Joe responded with haste. He heard his confession before some of the man's family members. The hospital staff was cooperative and arranged for Joe to use the whirlpool tub in the burn unit to immerse the candidate and complete his conversion (Romans 6:4). Everyone was happy. Since then, Joe has had the privilege of baptizing quite a few penitent persons under similar circumstances and has always had full cooperation of the hospital staff.

The church at Corner conducted no Vacation Bible School (VBS) annually, so I determined to drive our three children and three of their friends to another congregation, approximately 15 miles distant, to attend their VBS. We attended faithfully the entire week of the program. We did not know a picnic was planned following the last day of classes until one of the teachers casually asked me that last morning, "Are you planning to stay today for our picnic?"

"I have heard nothing about a picnic," I answered.

She said nothing further; nor did anyone else.

I did not mention anything to the children about the church picnic; but as we left, I announced my plans to prepare a picnic for all of them as soon as we reached home. Everyone was pleased to hear that announcement.

The careless treatment we received that week brought home to me how hurtful it can be to be excluded. And our children will tell you to this day how we taught them from their youth to be friendly with everyone, and always make a special effort to make visitors feel welcome in our congregation.

MORE SPECIAL MEMORIES, OUR CHILDREN AND OTHERS

Once when I was teaching VBS to a class of fourth-grade students in a neighboring congregation, one youngster interrupted the class with a question.

"Miss Pruett, where did the Ole Devil come from?"

I have always answered truthfully any questions posed. I confessed, "Honey, I do not know, but I'll find out and tell you tomorrow."

It took some searching the Bible that evening and night, but I had the answer ready for him as promised the following morning. (Satan was a fallen angel! Jesus said he saw him fall from heaven as lightning.) See Luke 10:18.

Also, when I was teaching fourth-grade youngsters at another congregation, the parents of a young lady in the class had recently granted their daughter the privilege of wearing pantyhose to worship on Sunday mornings. After the first few Sundays, she forgot to wear them. When she prayed in class that morning, she added a P.S. in childlike sincerity: Oh, please, God, don't ever let me forget again to wear my panty hose to church!"

* * *

I received much joy rearing our three children, interacting with them and observing their growing-up years. Several amusing incidents occurred during our years at Corner, which we can never forget.

Starr grew into an adorable child, as did all three of our children. She was clever at expressing herself and seemed always to have the right vocabulary to paint memorable word pictures. We were visiting friends one afternoon when the hostess asked me to describe the new kitchen countertops recently installed in our house. They were pink, splattered with gold and silver flecks.

My response was, "They have a soft pink background with…" and hesitated briefly, to think of how to describe the splotches.

Walking through the room at that moment, Starr sensed my hesitation. She immediately came to my rescue. "Mama, you know, they have freckles all over them."

Another time, when Starr was viewing something on an old television set a Christian brother gave us, she came running into the kitchen where I stood washing dinner dishes, and excitedly announced, "Mama, they are speaking a language on television that I don't understand. I think it is Spinach!"

One beautiful summer morning, I was busy cleaning the kitchen after overnight guests had left, so I instructed the girls to take their little brother outside in the backyard and care for him so I could finish tidying up the kitchen. They dutifully obeyed.

I kept a close eye on them, or so I thought, by looking every few minutes through the window over the kitchen sink, which faced the backyard. I failed to see them mounting Tony on the lower branch of a tree; but I was looking out the window just as he fell to the ground. I ran out the back door, frightened, thinking he might be seriously hurt.

When I picked him up, however, he was not even crying, just moaning slightly. Angel and Starr were sitting on higher branches and were so busy chattering they were unaware Tony had fallen; nor were they aware of my presence until I spoke.

"Who put your baby brother up in the tree?"

At that, both the girls looked down at me holding Tony close to my heart. Their eyes opened wide in astonishment.

After a few seconds Angel responded, "Mama, I put him up in this tree, but I have no idea how he got down!"

I could not bring myself to punish the girls, for their faces indicated complete surprise and honesty, and I knew they didn't realize the danger they had created. I explained to them Tony was too little to understand he should cling to branches; and, consequently, he had tumbled off. (Fortunately, the grass was a few inches high and had carpeted his fall.) I told them they must keep a closer watch on him in the future when he was in their care, until he was old enough to take care of himself. And they continued to help care for him for brief periods when necessary, with no other comparable incidents.

I BECOME A
STUDENT AGAIN

I had been out of high school three years when Joe and I married, but I had been on my own for many years, most of my life, in fact, and I was ready to marry. I did harbor a reservation, however; for I never forgot Mother's emphasis on the value of an education and her keen awareness of her own limitations. For these reasons, I subconsciously regretted not having completed a college degree prior to marriage, realizing it could end my days of formal schooling.

I cannot remember exactly when Joe and I agreed I should enroll in the University of Alabama Birmingham (UAB), which was then only an extension of the main campus in Tuscaloosa. (Due to its phenomenal growth, it soon became an independent campus.)

Mother volunteered to live with us so I might attend day classes. UAB's schedule allowed the students to complete semester hours' work during each quarter by lengthening each class period. I enrolled part time, attending class only two days a week, unwilling to be away from the children any longer than that. Thankfully, I received credit for almost all the quarter hours I had completed at FHC. Also, on those two days I had some free hours, and I was allowed to work for one of the professors, Richard Simmons, who was attending advanced courses at the main campus to complete requirements for a doctorate. Later I was asked to assist the faculty on registration days for each new term. This afforded me funds to pay college costs; plus, it provided me an opportunity to become better acquainted with faculty members, and many of the students as well.

I slowly advanced in my studies. At some point, one of my professors, Dr. John Coley, hired me to grade his language and literature papers. It was work I felt honored to perform, and it made me study even more diligently to ensure I graded papers accurately. I never heard any complaint from him, so I surely performed that job satisfactorily.

HELP ARRIVES

When I entered UAB, I had been out of high school for 14 years, and I was quite intimidated about becoming a student again. I was especially fearful of entering a college math class. Here again, the Lord provided my needs, not only in math but in two of my science courses. In that first math class, a younger student must have noticed my forlorn expression, for she came to sit beside me.

"Mrs. Pruett, would you like for me to help you with your math?" she inquired.

"Thank you, Lord," I silently prayed before responding, "Sure."

I soon learned she was a fine young Christian and willing to help me with any math problem.

As we became better acquainted, she often came to our house on Wednesdays and tutored me as necessary. She remained for dinner and then attended mid-week Bible study with us. She became such a blessing to us, and I believe she enjoyed her relationship with our family, along with our hospitality.

In my last math course, I was really lost at first. On the first test, five problems represented all we had studied thus far. Others must have been stumped too or thought they would be; for an answer sheet was circulated to the entire class. When it was handed to me, I passed it on to the person beside me without looking at it. After the test, I told the student who slipped the answer sheet to me I would rather fail the course than copy another's work.

Surely enough, I answered correctly only two of the five problems.

After the professor distributed the graded papers, she remarked to the class, "There are some dummies in this class. If you wish me to help you, be here at 8 a.m. Saturday morning, and I'll help you."

After class, I went to her desk and blurted, "I am one of the dummies you mentioned, so I'll be here Saturday morning!"

On Saturday, the professor patiently worked all morning with all who came at the appointed time, explaining how and why we could arrive at the correct answer to each of the five test problems, groundwork for solving future problems in the course.

For the remainder of the term I performed satisfactorily and earned a B, one of the few times I fell below the A for which I always strived. In fact, as soon as I could enroll in a full-time course load, once all the children were in school, my grades always placed me on the Dean's List, and I began to look forward to receiving his congratulatory letter at the close of each term. I remained at UAB until I had earned both a bachelor's and a master's degree.

God's angels came to my rescue in science class, too. Two of my courses required an extra four hours of lab work each week. The lab instructor told us to choose a lab partner with whom to work the entire term. In my 30s I was the oldest one in the class and was sometimes referred to as "Grandma" by my classmates. I sat frozen. I hadn't noticed the young man in the back of the room, also without a partner, when all selections had been otherwise completed.

Suddenly he appeared in the seat next to me and asked, "Mrs. Pruett, would you like to be my partner in lab work?"

I responded, "Sure," but only after I silently thanked God for him.

I do not recall his name, but we made a good pair and remained partners for both lab courses. He showed me how to look down a microscope and how to identify whatever specimens we studied. I worked diligently and earned high marks for my efforts; I'm sure my lab partner made high marks also. I have never ceased to be thankful for the help I received from him and the young lady who tutored me in my first math class. I have consequently been eager to help my students in any way possible during my later teaching years.

The idea of a God who created the earth and all that is in it was taboo at UAB, as I suppose had been the case in public universities for numerous decades. Among his initial instructions, the professor made clear to the class that the text taught evolution, and those students who held to the idea that God was the author of all things must answer exam questions according to the text if they expected to pass his course. I appreciated his warning; it caused me to study the text more diligently. When I answered questions on exams, I always made it clear that the text states thus and so, which implied my personal belief was otherwise. My answers satisfied the professor enough to earn a B on the text and an A in the lab course.

For my second course, I chose earth science; it was enlightening and interesting to learn more about the earth and its contents. Our professor scheduled two field trips, one to a marble mine/quarry in Sylacauga where I was truly captivated by what I saw and learned. First, I learned the purest (whitest) marble in the world is found there and is shipped all over the world. Secondly, I saw men carving an angel on each side of a small tombstone intended to grace a child's grave. I also saw chunks of marble in which pyrite was embedded. I learned, among other thing, pyrite is often mistaken for gold because of its bright gold metallic color.

Our second field trip was to visit a cut through a section of Red Mountain, where a Birmingham expressway was under construction. In the bowels of that mountain I found no fewer than two dozen aquatic specimens, many of which were entirely whole. (Were not these items another positive proof of the flood of Noah's days?) The professor quickly assured me I could identify as many of the samples as I could and mount them for my term project. Little did I suspect he would ask to keep my exhibit for himself after he assigned a huge A atop the finished project. I have not only wondered what became of it but more than that, I have regretted not keeping it for myself. It would have been a unique memento of my UAB school days, and a real Alabama treasure.

Mother remained with us for only that first school year, for I determined I would not attend college further if neither Joe nor I could manage to be at home with the children any time they were home. UAB offered evening classes, so Joe and I worked out a plan by which he would care for the children while I took evening classes.

The plan worked well, though I often arose at 4 a.m. to study three hours before waking the children, preparing their breakfast, and seeing them off to school. This routine continued until Tony entered kindergarten and was away the entire day, allowing me to become a full-time day student in my last year at UAB, the eleventh one. I have remarked a few times, in jest, UAB probably issued me both degrees to avoid my becoming a permanent student!

Mother and I cut out, pieced, and quilted by hand a 100% cotton quilt during those winter months on my weekdays at home. As a token of thanks for the help she gave us that school year, I later made a quilt entirely by hand and presented it to her.

ADDENDUM TO COLLEGE DAYS

While still working toward a second degree, I became a charter member of the UAB National Alumni Society (and later a lifetime member). I was active in the association as long as we lived in Birmingham and contributed articles to the *UAB Alumni Gazette*. As one thankful for the opportunity to receive an education, and a loyal graduate, Joe and I purchased season tickets to the home games of both the basketball and the football teams and formed a camaraderie with season-ticket holders seated near us.

One special honor I received during my years at UAB came thanks to the persistence of one of my professors, Dr. Elizabeth Blackwell, who would not accept a resounding "No" when she asked me to enter a contest on the dangers of drinking, sponsored by the Women's Christian Temperance Union (WCTU). I had no intention of doing so, for I had my hands more than full taking care of my family while still finding time to attend classes and prepare my homework.

I finally yielded to Dr. Blackwell's importunity and began my research. I included a great deal of pertinent information, including statistics on the result of drunkenness.

Each evening, after dinner, I left washing dishes and the girls' homework in Joe's hands, while I retired to the back bedroom, closed the door, and studied my presentation until I could recite it perfectly.

Though unknown to me until later, Tony, still a preschooler, was standing outside the bedroom door listening to me each time I rehearsed. One evening he pecked on the door, rushed into the room and exclaimed, "Mama, you missed a word!"

Obviously, he had mastered the speech before I did! But master it I did – and won both local and state honors. Before I had time to consider the consequences, the women of the WCTU sent me to Chicago to enter the national contest.

To my complete surprise, I won first place. Following the contest, I queried one of the judges as to how I won, for it seemed obvious to me that some of my opponents were better speakers than I. The judge explained that content counted 40 percent of the 100-point overall score, and I was the only contestant who scored a perfect 40 on it, raising my total score above all the others'.

My sponsors asked me to remain in Chicago an entire week and enter the international competition four days later. I declined, not wanting to be away from my family so long. I learned later I probably would have won that contest also, had I stayed, for the young man who won second place in the national contest garnered the international crown. Still, I never regretted returning to my family.

As Paul Harvey used to spin a five-minute "The Rest of the Story" on his daily afternoon radio broadcast, I have a "Rest…" to recount in connection with my Chicago trip. I had a night flight scheduled for my return to Birmingham. It was 10:30 p.m. when I left the Pick-Congress Hotel, where the contest was held, and walked across the street to the bus stop where the route to the airport began.

I was the sole passenger boarding there. After a few minutes, I became uncomfortable when I noticed the driver was not continuing his route but recircling the block. Shortly thereafter, he parked the bus on a narrow, dimly lit street, directly in front of a small bar whose front door stood open. Presently, he opened the bus door, turned to me, and asked, "Will you go in and have a drink with me?"

I tried to remain calm. "Thank you, Sir, but I think it best that I shouldn't, for I have just left the Pick-Congress Hotel where I gave a speech on the dangers of drinking."

The man said nothing more but proceeded to enter the bar. I saw him sitting on a bar stool, drinking, while I remained alone in the bus, frozen in fear and lifting up fervent prayers to God to get me home safely, contemplating what might happen after the driver had fortified himself with a drink.

After some minutes he reentered the bus, closed the door, and continued his route, collecting passengers along the way, eventually depositing us at the airport. Oh, how I thanked God for I know he was watching over me in a special way that night! The rest of my journey was uneventful, and I returned safely to my family in the early morning hours of the following day.

With the money I won in the contest, I purchased a set of Towle sterling, El Grandee pattern, and some additional serving pieces, a possession I otherwise would never have been able to own. This family treasure remains as beautiful as it was the day I bought it.

BIRMINGHAM AND CHELSEA YEARS (1967-99)

The Lord had different plans in mind for us, for the Cahaba Heights congregation in the Greater Birmingham area invited Joe to become the minister there in the late fall of 1966. After prayerful consideration, we accepted their offer. We sold our house and the eight acres surrounding it, immediately paid the remaining debt on the property, and moved into the comfortable three-bedroom brick parsonage next door to the church building.

Angel began third grade at Cahaba Heights School and Starr entered first grade. They made friends quickly both among the children of the congregation as well as at school and were happy in the new setting. The entire family quickly became acquainted with everyone and fit snugly into our work from the start. We continued what had been our practice from the start of Joe's first ministry, visiting the home of every congregant. Perhaps that explains why we always preferred working with small congregations; we declined a number of invitations to work with larger churches. We kept our commitment to treat everyone with respect and love, and to keep intimate Christian friendships as private as possible.

One of the first couples we met at Cahaba Heights (formerly New Merkel) were newlyweds, Joyce and John "Johnny" Vinsant, with whom we became instant friends. We also made friends with John's brother Albert and his wife Retha, also members of the congregation. Their three sons, Ky, Barry, and Al, also attended Cahaba Heights School. The boys frequently rode the school bus home with Angel and Starr and stayed for the afternoon when Retha took care of business out of town. Those friendships have endured through the years.

Both Albert and Johnny were firemen. Albert's work station was located nearby, and he often invited Joe there for a meal with all the employees, and he would give Joe a massage any time Joe was nursing a headache.

Albert had built up a successful painting and decorating business in Cahaba Heights on his off days, and Johnny was his top salesman. Albert sometimes subcontracted small jobs to Joe when he had time to do the work, so we were invited to their employee parties. I recall attending one of Albert's Christmas parties when another employee, an older gentleman, remarked to Joe he had never before had so much fun at any party where there were no alcoholic beverages served!

OUR WORK AT CAHABA HEIGHTS

Joe and I never permitted our three children to accompany us on house visits unless they were specifically invited; but sometimes the four of us tagged along when Joe needed to make hospital visits, always carrying a few children's books along. We sat in the lobby, with Tony in my lap with Angel and Starr perched one on each side of the chair, and spent time reading stories while "Daddy" made his visits to patients.

Joe soon had a faithful visiting partner in one of the young men of the congregation who idolized him. Any time this young man was available, he was knocking on our door, ready to make home and hospital visits with Joe.

Once, when Joe conducted a home Bible study with a young lady, May Wesson (whose mother and siblings worshipped with the Cahaba Height congregation), the children and I went along, as the classes were held each Saturday afternoon during the summer when I could keep them entertained and playing in the yard without disturbing the study. The teenage girl converted at the conclusion of the study. Years later Joe was asked to officiate at her wedding.

Twenty-seven years later, May's father, Raymond Wesson, called Joe, seeking assistance in his conversion. He had listened to Joe's teaching his daughter so long ago and believed it then but was not ready until lately to repent of his prior sinful years and surrender himself to the Lord.

Joe arranged for Raymond to confess his faith in Jesus Christ before his family and others and submit to the rite of baptism. What a wonderful day for his entire family! Raymond proved to be a faithful Christian. Besides talking to others of his faith, he contributed to the church far above his means. His conversion brought the family together again, and they enjoyed many joyful reunions. We were always invited to their gatherings. Years later Joe was called to officiate at Raymond's funeral.

In addition, Joyce and Johnny had no children until after 16 years of marriage, so Joyce worked as a secretary in downtown Birmingham. Johnny's fireman work schedule meant Joyce spent many nights alone. She became fond of our children, particularly Tony; and the children reciprocated that fondness.

Joyce volunteered to mind the children at least one evening a week, allowing Joe and me to visit church members at home or in the hospital, or teach private Bible lessons.

Usually we knew ahead of time which evening Joyce was coming, so she could drive straight to our house from her downtown office and enjoy a made-from-scratch dinner with us before Joe and I left. But one late afternoon she appeared at our door without our being apprized of her coming. As a stay-at-home mom, I had earlier become the community baby sitter. That was one of the days I had six children under foot, in addition to my three, and general pandemonium reigned. When I opened the door, Joyce narrowly escaped being hit by the broom with which the children had been playing, when it fell across the door.

She noticed the look of surprise on my face. I did not immediately invite her in, but she was unfazed.

After a few seconds, she said, "I'm here to stay with the children, so you and Joe can go visiting."

I responded that she would have difficulty getting into the house, for I had there a total of nine children and did not know when six of them would be called for, so probably we could not go visiting that evening.

I've wondered whether Joyce had smelled the huge pot of chili on our stove, for she quickly removed her glasses and offered the following disclaimer, "Ruby, I'm blind as a bat without my glasses, and I cannot see any disorder in your house."

She gave me no instant to remonstrate but just walked in. The six children were soon fetched, and our family shared the chili with "Miss Joyce," after which Joe and I went on our calls.

Joyce assisted Angel and Starr if they needed help with their homework; bedtime for all three children was 8:30. Many years later, Joyce confessed to me the girls always retired at 8:30, but she permitted Tony to stay up to see the *Carol Burnett Show* (which came on at 9), since he wanted to, and he didn't have to rise early for school. She said each time the audience laughed, Tony laughed along, though he surely had no understanding of the meaning of Carol Burnett's antics and remarks!

I asked Tony, by then a grown man, whether he remembered Miss Joyce's having allowed him to stay up late after his older sisters were sent to bed when she babysat all of them.

Without catching a breath, he responded, "Yes, and I watched the *Carol Burnett Show!*"

And all that time, Angel and Starr never squealed on either Joyce or Tony.

Once, Joyce approached Angel and said she wished to buy me a birthday gift and had thought of giving me a pair of house shoes. Without a moment's hesitation, Angel squelched the idea.

"Oh no, Miss Joyce. My mama never wears anything around the house but Daddy's old ragged socks!"

Unfortunately, three of the four Vinsant friends have already taken their leave of this earth. Our entire family were grieved to lose such dear friends – Albert, Johnny, and Joyce – from the dreaded disease, cancer. All three died too soon; and Joyce, the youngest of them, had been almost a daughter to us. She died from inoperable malignant brain tumors. Joe officiated at two of the three funerals.

* * *

No one could have been more friendly or hospitable toward us than Boyd and Trishel Drake, whom we met at the Vinemont congregation in Cullman County. Diversified farming had made them successful, and they shared their bounty in numerous ways. During both our summers there, I loaded the children in our Volkswagen on several occasions and drove the 65 miles to their farm, where we helped the family gather butter beans, corn, green beans, peas, and sweet potatoes, which Boyd took to Birmingham, where he had long since established a ready market. We never accepted pay, but Boyd always gave us a supply of the various vegetables we helped to harvest, to can or freeze for winter's use.

Years later, Joe was called to officiate at their funerals. Boyd died first, followed soon afterward by Trishel.

One of their grandsons approached me after one of the funerals and asked me whether I remembered helping his Grandpa pick peas on his farm.

"Of course!" I responded.

He then said he used to look at me occasionally while all of us were picking peas and noted that I always wore a smile on my face. My smile puzzled him, he confessed, for he could not understand how anyone could manage a smile in the pea patch!

I replied, "I was happy; I grew up on a farm where I picked peas for many years." Doing farm work reminded me of my childhood; plus, I was happy to help your grandparents harvest their crops."

We forged many other friendships at congregations we served, as well as in other settings. John and Robbie Kivette at Columbiana, and Richard and Beth Glasgow. Both couples lived on a cove of the Coosa River. John always hosted an annual fish fry for the entire congregation, with fish he caught on the river.

Richard was one of Joe's converts. He and Beth generously invited us to stay in their lake house many times when we returned to the area following our 1999 move to Tennessee.

We taught our children to value friendships and to never allow the breakup of a friendship to be their fault. For many of years of their childhood, they were required to learn a memory verse each week. One such verse was I Samuel 18:1, which speaks of the close friendship/love that existed between David and Jonathan. Their souls were "knit together," and "Jonathan loved David as his own soul." We feel the same toward many whose friendship we have enjoyed.

MORE ACCIDENTS AND MORE ILLNESSES

Our family has not been without illnesses and other trials.
In giving birth to our firstborn, Angel, I was left with a permanently damaged muscle with which I've had to deal throughout my life.

Tony seemed inclined toward accidents. He severed 80% of one of his index fingers during his third year while trying to close a sliding glass door. Another time he climbed upon a small night table and fell as he was trying to reach a high window directly above it, almost pulverizing his lower lip and mouth. Unfortunately, his proneness to accidents has continued in his adult life; but so far, he has managed to recover from them all and quickly return to his busy lifestyle.

Before Starr's second school year ended, she was struck with meningitis, which almost claimed her life. She had a stiff, swollen neck and unmanageable headache, accompanied by high fevers. She could neither eat nor drink, but vomited everything, even water, and was delirious. Her body seemed to melt away so quickly she could have modeled as a stick figure! When she was admitted to Children's Hospital in Birmingham, she was placed in isolation; Joe and I were the only ones permitted to visit. Her attending physician said she would most likely be left with brain impairment – if she recovered.

I gave her up in my heart and was at peace even though before I was tested, I had always thought I could not bear to lose one of my children. God be praised, she eventually recovered with no brain impairment (?);

but she suffered headaches for a long time afterward, and she was left with a residual condition that causes her to lose consciousness intermittently. Neurologists identify this as a kind of seizure, which requires her to take medication the rest of her life.

I praise God for giving her back to us. It has caused me to think of Abraham and his son Isaac. Though God spared Isaac, it was to Abraham as though God raised him from the dead, for Abraham had already given Isaac to God in his heart. We have always been especially thankful for her recovery; she has brought so much joy to her father and me.

During Starr's convalescence, her classmates wrote her notes, which we treasured. A young lad in her class who lived nearby (and was quite attracted to Starr but was of no interest to her), wrote the following: "Starr, I sure do miss chasing you around the school yard!"

Later he rode his pony to our house one afternoon after school and knocked at our door.

When I answered, he blurted out, "How's Starr, Miss Pruett?"

I responded that Starr was still in the process of recovery.

That answer provoked his comment, "Ain't that a shame!"

While Starr was hospitalized, Tony was scheduled to appear on a Saturday-morning television program, "Romper Room," with Miss ____ at Birmingham's WBRC. Though Starr was close to death and required either Joe or me to be at her side at all times, we were determined Tony should make that special once-in-a-lifetime appointment. I do not recall exactly how we managed, but with the assistance of brethren and friends, Tony arrived at the television station in good time and performed well among his peers.

Sometime later, Starr was invited to spend the weekend with a classmate. We permitted her to go, though both Joe and I harbored indistinct reservations.

The family spent the weekend on their horse farm in an adjoining county. Late on Saturday afternoon, one of the parents assisted in saddling up the girls to go horseback riding.

The one Starr mounted was quite a frisky one. Within minutes, it had thrown her, and she landed on the gnarled roots of a tree. Both of her arms were crushed, but her friend's parents notified us only after they had taken Starr to the hospital in Birmingham for x-rays and treatment. Even then, all the circumstances surrounding the accident were not made clear to us, as Starr later revealed.

We hurried to the hospital only to learn Starr's arms were already in casts from her fingers to above her elbows. The family reluctantly revealed the multiple fractures to the right arm were reset, but the left arm was so crushed that the bones could not be reset. The surgeon stated those bones would gradually reunite on their own, and the resulting misshapen bones would, ever so slowly, abrade until the arm would reshape itself and look normal.

Starr did gradually heal, but she missed weeks of school and had to be cared for completely during that time, unable to manipulate her arms.

* * *

During the 1980s I received a third-degree burn on my right foot after dropping a huge blackberry cobbler on it while removing the cobbler from the oven. Though experiencing excruciating pain, I attempted to continue my work and home routine until my foot became infected. Forced to see our family physician, he bandaged the foot, gave me medication, and threatened hospitalization unless I agreed to stay off my feet for a few days and keep the affected one elevated all the while. I obeyed and was forced to miss some days of work.

It was months before I was healed sufficiently to wear regular shoes again, and several weeks until I could wrap my entire foot and get it into an oversized rubber garden boot. If you can imagine such a sight, I began wearing those garden boots to worship, paired with my usual Sunday dress and hat. Though I regretted having to do so, I cared little about how I might appear to anyone.

Sometime later, one of the dear sisters in the congregation could not resist telling me about comments she had heard. "Ruby, I admired you for coming to church in your rubber boots just as soon as you could after your accident. I did not talk about you like some of the other sisters did!"

That revelation caused me to think about just how ridiculous I must have looked. I read some time ago that it is a gracious thing to ignore an insult! I merely smiled at the comment and stated I was thankful no one took a picture of me in my Sunday ensemble.

MORE CHILDREN'S ACTIVITIES

Joe and I wanted the children to engage in wholesome activities both secular and religious; hence, some questionable activities were denied, but we made every effort to replace them with those which promoted soundness of body and mind. All three children made friends easily, and they knew they were free to invite friends into our home any time. Consequently, there were always children visiting, many of whom were overnight guests.

We remained heavily involved in all their activities – church, home, and school – until they grew up and left the nest. We always attended their sports activities. During the years I was teaching, I always managed to visit the children's school at least once a year and have lunch with them, even when they were attending three different schools, and confer with their teachers. Also, as soon as they were old enough, all three became Scouts. I became a Troop Leader at first and later a Troop Organizer. Joe worked with the Boy Scouts as soon as Tony was old enough to become one. Tony still recalls his and his father's memorable camping weekend with Tony's troop.

During our tenure in Birmingham, there were several stage performances of *The Nutcracker Suite*. One free performance was offered to parents of school-age children each year. Neither Joe nor I had ever seen ballet performed. We decided to take our children at the risk of censorship from some of our brethren. We were so mesmerized with its beauty and artistry that we attended several years thereafter. Thereafter, I chaperoned a group of my students to the performance each year, for as long as I taught at Chelsea School.

* * *

I have long been an admirer of Norman Rockwell's positive portrayals of life in America. One time, when 80 of his original oils were on a national tour, Liberty National Insurance Company hosted a 60-day exhibit of them in its downtown Birmingham headquarters. Though it took considerable coaxing to interest Starr, she and I were privileged to view them.

As we left the building, Starr said to me, "Mother, thank you for making me come with you today!"

That "thank you" richly repaid me for my insistence she go with me, against her will, for I realized she was inspired with Rockwell's art work.

* * *

Throughout their grammar-school years, both Angel and Starr had lovely Jewish friends, Ellen and Holly respectively, daughters of Leonard and Gertrude Hackman.

The first time Holly stayed overnight with us was a Friday. Come Saturday morning, I was thoughtlessly preparing our usual Saturday-morning breakfast of bacon, eggs, biscuits, and gravy, a Southern tradition (one we continue to observe whenever all our family is together).

When Holly smelled the bacon frying, she jumped out of bed and came running into the kitchen. "Now, Mrs. Pruett, you know I can't be eating that bacon!"

I apologized profusely and told Holly I knew better but wasn't thinking properly. I assured her I would prepare her a breakfast of her choice and would never fry bacon again when she came for a visit.

Holly surely communicated her experience to her parents, and I know all was forgiven, for we became good friends with her family and visited back and forth in each other's homes. I even once sewed a costume for Ellen, with which both Ellen and her mother were delighted!

Once, we were invited to Thanksgiving dinner at the Hackmans. Tony ate roasted turkey until he was overstuffed, and I was a little embarrassed and made some sort of remark to him after his third or fourth serving.

Leonard quickly came to his rescue, saying, "Ruby, don't worry about Tony. He will never become sick from eating turkey."

Unfortunately for us, Leonard was eventually promoted, requiring a move to his company's headquarters in New York City, so they left Birmingham permanently! Friendship like theirs is rare, and we feel blessed that our paths crossed in life.

* * *

Starr also had a friend in junior-high school named Helen Pruet. They did a brief skit on stage at school one day which garnered much laughter from their audience.

Helen remarked, "Starr, did you know my father is a doctor, and I can be sick for nothing?"

Starr responded, "That's nothing, Helen; my father is a preacher, and I can be good for nothing!"

* * *

Tony was quite lonely when Starr entered first grade at Cahaba Heights; to compensate, he became quite an imaginative child. One particularly beautiful and clear day in the early spring, he was with me in the backyard as I pinned our wash to the clothesline. Two sides of our yard were surrounded by trees, and I was enjoying listening to the birds chirp songs from their perch on the tree branches.

Momentarily Tony came running up to me, exclaiming, "Mama, the birds are singing!"

I responded, "Yes, son, they are welcoming spring."

Tony walked away from me, but after a moment or two, he came running back with a second exclamation. "Mama, the birds are having a birthday party, but they forgot to bring a birthday cake!"

That day I locked in my heart the feeling that, even at an early age, children can conceive of the beauty of God's natural world and the renewal of life with the coming of spring each year.

Later Tony began to entertain himself with his imaginary friend, David. Tony and David both worked together and played together. I had to make David's lunch every day the same as Tony's; I had to be careful at times not to step on David or sit on him at the table; they sometimes had a job and went to work together outside. They went to worship together. They even sometimes brushed their teeth together at the same lavatory! They remained steady friends until Tony entered first grade; at that time, David evaporated just as quickly as he had magically materialized.

A FAMILY JOB

One day after we had been serving the Cahaba Heights church for some time, we received a call asking if we would be interested in cleaning the church building weekly. (The prior janitor had been dismissed for improper behavior.)

We lost no time responding, "Yes." We lived next door, we needed the money, and it would not interfere with Joe's regular work.

We talked with the children about it. We told them we could give them no money for home chores, since for a family to function well, every member should assume some responsibility without expectation of pay. However, if they were willing to help us clean the building, we could give them a portion of the pay. All agreed.

We divided the work details. Angel and Starr must prepare the classrooms for vacuuming and put them back in order after they were cleaned and dust the pews. Tony was responsible for preparing the auditorium for vacuuming and replacing all hymnals in the pew racks. I cleaned the bathrooms and the huge nursery window, while Joe vacuumed the entire building and cleaned the water fountain, leaving it dry and as shiny as new. Angel remembers that later Dad showed her how to vacuum the classrooms, which then became a part of her weekly list of chores.

Before we started, we showed the children how to do everything. All took their work seriously and did an outstanding job. Though only four years old, Tony never had to be shown a second time how to arrange the hymnals, and he carefully picked up every scrap of paper or other debris on the auditorium floor.

After each weekly cleaning, we gave Angel and Starr $1 each and 50 cents to Tony. It was theirs to spend or save as they wished. We purchased Tony a piggy bank, and he filled it with his 50-cent coins. I still have a mental image of the pleasure he took in dropping his "big" piece of money into his bank each "payday."

I do not recall the amount we were paid, but Joe and I decided we would save it, as we had been living without it and could still do so. It was the first time we had one cent over and above bare living expenses, and both of us felt the need to begin saving toward the future, if only modestly.

A PAINFUL "PAY LODE"

Life is sometimes full of surprises. We were happy and blessed in the Cahaba Heights congregation until one Sunday morning, during a Bible class, as Joe read from Matthew 19:3-9, he began to discuss what Jesus says about marriage between a man and a woman and the consequences of marriage and divorce. One of the influential brothers, who had served in WWII, voiced a strong belief that adultery did not count in times of war! We had never heard such an interpretation, and a lively discussion ensued; but we thought little more about it.

We were totally unaware anything was afoot until a few weeks later, in early 1971, when Joe was handed a letter asking him to resign immediately. It was signed by a majority of one of the men. The letter acknowledged Joe had never preached anything but the truth of God's word; the resignation request was made to keep peace within the congregation! The letter shocked and pricked our hearts to the core!

As soon as it was known Joe had received the letter, the brethren who had refused to sign the document immediately faced their opposing brethren with a strong condemnation. They declared their opposition to firing a man whose very opponents admitted he had preached only the truth of God's word. Further, no one had brought forth any charge of misconduct against him, nor any member of his family. They asked whether "preaching the truth" constituted sufficient cause to fire a minister.

When nothing persuaded the instigators to drop their request for Joe's resignation, they agreed to the other brethren's bold demands (i.e., the minister's salary must continue until the end of May – five full months – so his daughters could complete their school term; nor must the family be uprooted suddenly, but rather be permitted to live in the parsonage until that same time).

As a result, Joe received full salary for the time specified, and our family continued to live in the minister's home. We lost no respect or standing in the community, and the income seemed almost a "pay lode" for us, because Joe began filling the pulpit in an adjoining county within two weeks, and we were able to use the extra pay for a considerable down payment on the purchase of a home from a family in the congregation who was building a house in a new subdivision nearby. We had previously studied with the husband of that family, which culminated in his conversion.

Still, it was a painful blow, over which I shed many tears. While we made every attempt to keep the children's home life normal, both Angel and Starr were old enough to realize something was amiss, which pained us.

We learned after the fact that the letter seeking Joe's resignation had been circulated to every family in the congregation and asked for the signature of the head of the family, surreptitiously, until it finally reached the slim majority of one vote. Looking back, my conviction is that none of the brethren could find wrongdoing by anyone in our family and they really regretted having caused such a problem; but the leaders could not humble themselves sufficiently to recant their actions.

In time, almost all the brethren whose signatures were attached to that fateful letter apologized profusely for their actions and confessed they felt pressured to do so, although they had no complaint against us. We freely forgave them, and our friendships have endured. We hold no ill will in our hearts toward any of them. However, the experience brought about a serious and permanent change in our lives.

A New Beginning

Joe and I did much prayerful soul searching during the months of our transition. Regardless of where he served, and whatever salary he received, we lived within our means throughout the years.

During this period, Joe determined he would remain in the ministry, as he had early in life dedicated himself to do; in order never to place our family in such jeopardy again, however, he would embark upon secular work. Past the awkward adjustment of our move from Norway to Alabama, we had already begun to feel deeply rooted in Alabama, and we never gave a moment's thought to leaving the state.

We remained in the area for an additional 27 years and our fondness for Alabama has never diminished. Joe received long-term invitations from churches (i.e., from two-plus years to a period of 11 years), covering well over 20 years, altogether. Those congregations include Vinemont in Cullman County, and Montevallo, Columbiana, and Bear Creek, in Shelby County. In addition, he filled the pulpit at many other places for shorter periods of time wherever there was a need; these stints lasted from a few Sundays to several months, depending on their needs: Examples include substituting for a minister who was away from his pulpit for a long-term recovery from a brain malignancy, substituting for a minister who did mission work in India for an entire summer, and preaching for a congregation several months while the flock awaited the coming of their new minister.

During the brief periods when Joe wasn't engaged for the weekend, we worshipped with one of two congregation in the Greater Birmingham area. Joe also served as an elder in two congregations during our years in Alabama.

JOE'S SECULAR WORK

In the meantime, Joe was not without secular work. That kept us busy, for the brethren in some of the places we served in adjoining counties wanted us to be in their area for the entire weekend, after having worked at a secular job Monday through Friday. Joe's secular employment included stints with two insurance companies and a manufacturing Company.

With one of the companies, we were invited to a three-day weekend at a popular upscale vacation spot near Mobile. We could choose from among varied activities during the day; in the evenings we were expected to gather for cocktails at 7, followed by a 9 p.m. dinner hour. Joe and I skipped the cocktail gathering after the first night because the drinking far exceeded social drinking. During the two-hour dinner, the entire party, except Joe and me, continued to drink until the women began swapping their own husbands' laps for the laps of other men, and the men clasped their arms tightly around them. Joe and I had no desire to participate in that kind of recreation, so we excused ourselves each evening when the exchanging of spouses began and returned to our room. Before we returned home, Joe had already decided that company's employment was not the right fit for him; neither of us has ever regretted his immediate resignation.

Eventually Joe established a cleaning business broader than the Cahaba Heights church. It worked well, as long as we two could manage it in the evenings, but we had to abandon it after being called and cursed a number of times when people we had employed failed to show up without giving advance notice.

The ancient van in which we hauled our cleaning equipment often broke down on us. Late one night, we were driving home at 1 a.m., exhausted after having worked all day, followed by several hours of cleaning. Joe was behind me in the van, and I was keeping a lookout for him through my rearview mirror, in case he broke down again. It wasn't long before I lost sight of him while going up and down hills and around curves; I drove on a short distance, peering through my rearview mirror all the while, hoping all was well, and Joe would reappear.

Suddenly a policeman appeared and pulled me over.

I gave my name and produced my driver's license as requested.

After viewing it, he asked, "Are you Mrs. Pruett? 'Yes, Sir," I responded.

"Are you drunk?" was his next question.

I became no little upset at that inquiry and declared, "Sir, I have heard there is a test you can give to determine whether I am drunk. Please give me that test and you can determine for yourself if that is the case."

He proceeded to ask why I was weaving and added, "There are many drunk women out at that time of night looking for a man!"

At that statement, I became somewhat furious. "I am looking for a man, my husband!" Then somewhat more calmly, I explained the circumstances.

At that point, Joe drove up, exited the van and came running over to me.

"What happened? Are you all right, honey?"

I pointed to the policeman. "This man thinks I am drunk and looking for a man because he saw me weaving."

In truth, the policeman probably did see me swerve when I was looking so intently through the rearview mirror for more than a glance in my effort to locate Joe.

Still Joe confirmed my story, proving I was telling the truth. At that point, the policeman let us go.

Thereafter I received some teasing about whether the elders should be notified that I had been stopped for drunken driving!

One hot, sweltering summer Saturday, after the children were all gone, I did not accompany Joe on our Saturday cleaning job, owing to having so many household chores.

Joe returned home in the afternoon, exhausted and dripping with perspiration. As he entered the house, he held up his hands to me and exclaimed, "Honey, just look at these work-worn hands! I'm so afraid someday I'll start preaching like a janitor and janitoring like a preacher!"

Sometime later, Joe formed his own small painting company. Most of his work was subcontract work for our friend Albert, whose company had long since established a reputation for honesty and excellent work. He continued in this work until we moved to Crossville, Tennessee, in 1999.

MY PROFESSION

Though I remained a student at UAB until I earned a Master's Degree, I was employed to teach English at Chelsea School in Shelby County as soon as I earned a B.A. in the spring of 1971. Each year I was loaded with large classes. During my infrequent free periods, I was often asked to keep study hall. In addition, I served as an officer in the PTA and often scheduled speakers at monthly meetings. I took a turn at working in one capacity or another at the evening sports events. I sponsored the high-school cheerleaders for a year or two. I regularly invited professional people to speak to my classes in their subject area, and established a Junior Honor Society, Chelsea's first. I scheduled field trips for students that related to and reinforced their studies.

We spent an entire day visiting the School for the Blind and Deaf in Talladega after we finished reading the novels, *Light A Single Candle* and *Gift of Gold*, by Beverly Butler, which chronicled a young girl's difficulties after losing her sight due to illness. Upon correspondence with the author, we learned the novel was largely the story of her life. Though blind, she had overcome her problems and became a college instructor and a writer.

Another field trip took us to Birmingham for a visit with Mr. Charley Boswell. Boswell had been a professional baseball player when he was drafted into WWII. He was wounded during the war and lost his eyesight, ending his chosen career. Though despondent for a long period of time, with the encouragement of a professional golfer, he became a champion golfer for the blind and garnered 27 national and international trophies. In addition, he established a successful business in Birmingham.

I had found Boswell's autobiography, *Now I See*, in the Chelsea School library and determined it was a story that could encourage anyone, for he detailed how he eventually overcame his limiting and tortuous handicap and turned it into a success story. I read the book aloud to my eighth-grade students. After much class discussion, through the students' interest and my efforts, Mr. Boswell gave permission for some of my students to interview him.

Three students were chosen to accompany me. They brought a list of interview questions made up of a composite of questions submitted by the students. A more pleasant and unostentatious man I have never met!

At the conclusion of the interview, he spoke of his friendship with the Bob Hope and other famous persons, making each of us feel as if we were in the presence of royalty! Then with the guiding hand of his secretary, he inscribed his signature on our library book, which we wisely had brought along with us.

As we started to exit his office, he said, "Mrs. Pruett, I am playing golf this afternoon at Sylacauga. Could I ride with you to Chelsea? You can drop me off at Lloyd's restaurant there, and someone else will carry me the rest of the way."

"Of course!" I replied.

My three students crowded in the back seat of my car without a murmur. Though possessed of a large frame, Mr. Boswell hopped into the front seat of my little Volkswagen Beetle as easily and gracefully as if climbing into a limousine. Along the 30-minute ride, he spoke freely and kindly in conversation with the youngsters and me. When we arrived at Lloyd's, someone was already there to meet him. It made me wonder whether he had pre-planned his afternoon's travels.

I can only hope Mr. Boswell was as impressed with my well-behaved students as all of us were impressed with him, yea, inspired. They gave a report of the interview and consequent car ride to their classmates the following day.

At the end of the year, I regularly permitted all my students to evaluate me – the only teacher at Chelsea School who did so. All three of the youngsters who had made that memorable appointment with me wrote that the interview and ride with Mr. Boswell was the highlight of their school year!

* * *

Mother was not a professional in the worldly sense, but she was a bright and accomplished woman in her own way – especially considering she never finished fourth grade. Once, while she was visiting us, I invited her to call on one of my junior-high classes and allow the students to interview her.

"Oh, no, I couldn't do that," she insisted. "I wouldn't know what to say."

I knew better.

I made the arrangements with the principal and had the students primed to ask her questions about her young life, prior to her parents' death, and how she coped as an orphan. I placed a rocking chair beside my desk for her and rushed to fetch her from our recently purchased house in Chelsea, a mile from the school.

Within a few minutes of taking her seat, she warmed up to her task, became animated, and was expressing herself freely. She told of her life on the farm in Graves County, Kentucky, where her father ran a sawmill and a grist mill, in addition to farming tobacco, wheat, and corn. Afterward, she told of her difficult and lonely life after both parents died, causing the siblings to be separated permanently.

The students seemed mesmerized; she connected with them with such ease that they listened with rapt attention. By the end of the period, they had become fond enough of her to give her a big hug as they exited the classroom. Some even called her Mama Yates – the name by which all her grandchildren knew her. The mental picture of that event is imprinted on my mind and is one of my favorite memories.

* * *

Years after I resigned from Chelsea School, I tutored a first grader whose mother had been one of my students at Chelsea. He came on the day of my birthday. During the session I told him it was my birthday. He insisted I tell him my age, but I repeatedly told him I was old and my age must be kept a big secret.

His curiosity aroused, he would not be appeased.

I yielded with the words, "If you promise me you will never tell anyone, I'll whisper it to you."

"Oh, yes, Ma'am," he quickly agreed.

Then I whispered my age in his ear. "Fifty years old."

At that revelation, his eyes enlarged, and with a puzzled and surprised look, he blurted, "I wouldn't tell it either if I were that old!"

Especially dear are the times former students came to me after I left Chelsea School to say how much they appreciated my teaching them.

One former student recognized me in a group a few years later, walked up to me, offered his hand, and proclaimed, "Mrs. Pruett, I used to get mad at you when you corrected my English papers, but as I was earning a degree at Alabama (the University of Alabama is always referred to simply as "Alabama"), I thought of you many times and came to appreciate your strict teaching of grammar. It made my classes there much easier. Thank you!"

Another incident occurred fifteen years after I resigned from Chelsea School. Joe and I arrived a little early for a wedding rehearsal at which Joe was scheduled to officiate the following day. We popped into Lloyd's for a cup of coffee while waiting.

Four young men, none of whom I recognized, soon came in and sat in a booth near us. One of them was reading a book. He obviously recognized me, for shortly he sprang over to our table.

"You're Mrs. Pruett, aren't you?"

"Yes," I replied.

He identified himself as a former student, then stated, "You are the only person who ever read to me in my entire life, and now I am an insatiable reader," and pointed to the book in his hand.

We recalled some of the books we'd read aloud in class during his junior-high years, including *Now I See*, *Shane*, *Ole Yeller*, *Light A Single Candle*, and *Anne Frank*. I told him how glad I was to see him and how proud I was to know our reading aloud in class had made a permanent impression on him. Influencing youngsters in such a positive way is the goal, or should be the goal, of any teacher of youth.

* * *

Before resigning from Chelsea School, I applied for employment with the federal government and with BellSouth. After passing a professional federal examination, I was offered employment as a Taxpayer Service Representative, beginning at pay grade 5! Though he said nothing, I sensed Joe preferred I work for BellSouth, so I accepted BellSouth's offer at a much lower pay scale. I began as a Special Clerk and ended as an Assistant Staff Manager at BellSouth Human Resources Inc. and enjoyed my work there immensely.

* * *

During the late 1980s, I knew Mother was experiencing the evening of her life, and her evening would soon turn to night. I wanted to spend as much time with her as possible and be of any assistance I could. I felt strongly the urge to help Mother, the one who had exercised the greatest positive influence on my life and whom I admired above every other person in the world! I accepted weekend work at BellSouth for several years and drove the seven-hour trip to Obion almost weekly. While there, I cooked, laundered, cleaned, washed windows, mowed her small lawn – everything pertaining to her household maintenance. In addition, I taxied her grocery shopping, to doctors' appointments, to the drugstore for her prescriptions, kept her bills paid on time, and any other errand she wrote on her list, for she soon began to keep a list ready for me at all times.

Not only that, but I brought her alfalfa tablets by bottles of 1,000 each, purchased from a health-food store in Birmingham. Mother believed them healthful and took several daily.

I finally thought to ask the clerk what alfalfa tablets were good for.

He looked at me as though I should already know, obviously thinking I was the one who had been using them for so long. After a few seconds, he composed himself and answered, "Ma'am, that depends on what ails you."

After three and a half years, I returned to full-time work at BellSouth because two older siblings sold Mother's house in Obion and moved her into a tiny apartment in Dyersburg, where she failed to thrive – as is often the case when older people are forced into a different setting in their old age, accompanied with infirmities.

She soon fell and broke one hip. During her recovery, she suffered another broken hip. At that point, she was placed in a nursing home, where she lived the remainder of her life. She had been seen sitting in the chair beside her bed, crocheting an item for someone just hours before death occurred – an enviable way for death to claim anyone.

* * *

It was good to return to full-time work at BellSouth, but in 1991 the company extended its Voluntary Enhanced Early Retirement (VEER) offer to certain management personnel. This provided some valuable incentives, but only a meager pension. I was only 58 and had hoped to remain in the workforce at least until age 65. However, I knew when a company offers retirement, it is usually best to accept it, for it typically foretells a planned downsizing. Shortly after my retirement, my department was contracted to an outside vendor. Not many years hence, AT&T purchased the entire Bell system.

The Company feted me with a large, festive – and altogether memorable – retirement party. Our vice president, Mal Hutchins, attended and praised my writing skills to the audience. My operations manager, David Bertanzetti, related his dislike of my correcting his letters. He said he soon learned never to come to my desk and complain, however; for I would always remove my language book from its shelf, turn to the appropriate chapter and read aloud the applicable grammar rule. My immediate manager told of my teaching her young daughters to crochet. And when my close work associate, Teresa Bunn, sang, "Forever Friends," rivulets of tears flowed down the faces of many of the guests gathered there.

In addition to the multitude of telephone employees, several relatives and friends – some local, others far flung – attended my retirement party. I was particularly thankful all the leftover food was packaged and sent home with me, for 17 relatives in attendance spent that night with us after the party! I was so exhausted I could never have provided for them otherwise.

The following year, BellSouth employed me to recast and soften several hundred proprietary letters, from my home. Later that same year, I was also engaged to teach groups of company employees business letter-writing skills. I received a great deal of gratification for being called on to do this work, for it made me realize the Company recognized my work ethic and honesty, as well as my ability and skills in these areas.

* * *

A year prior to my retirement from BellSouth, I was accepted as a part-time evening instructor at the Birmingham campus of Faulkner University (FU), a Christian school whose main campus is in Montgomery, Alabama. Thus, I became an adjunct instructor a year prior to my leaving BellSouth. I continued to teach at FU for 10 years, until we moved to Crossville Tennessee. in 1999. I taught developmental reading, English composition, English literature, and beginning speech. I also taught some off-campus classes for the Alabama National Guard, under contract to FU for furthering the education of its members. In addition, I was one of the instructors interviewed when FU applied for – and was granted – membership in the prestigious Southern Association of Colleges and Universities.

A few years before our move to Crossville, Birmingham's largest newspaper organization, the *Birmingham News*, contacted me, offering me occasional work as a freelance journalist, for they needed someone to contribute occasional articles for an insert in their Sunday newspaper. I have long since come to believe painting mental word pictures is the highest form of art, so that work was sheer joy, and I regretted having to resign from it and FU, once we decided to accept Angel's invitation to move to Crossville.

Along with this work, I continued to teach both ladies' and children's Bible classes regularly.

SOCIAL ACTIVITIES

Besides preparing large Sunday dinners almost every week, I hosted many parties, showers, and teas in our home for friends and relatives, congregants and others, wherever Joe served as minister.

In addition, we were included in groups who enjoyed various social activities. We often gathered on Friday evenings to attend a dinner theater or to play games. One Friday evening I returned home from work and prepared dinner for my family and two other young couples, three of whom were my teaching associates at Chelsea, after which we played cards. My guests were still enjoying their game of Rook when the clock struck 11.

I said, "My friends, it's nearing my bedtime."

One of the young teachers responded, "Oh, Mrs. Pruett, please don't make me go home now. I'm having too much fun!"

Though exhausted, I held my peace and the game continued.

For many of our Birmingham years, we were part of a Christian Birthday Club. Members took turns hosting monthly gatherings where all enjoyed a shared dinner and fun, ending always by singing hymns. We bonded closely and always stood ready to help one another. So many of us gathered at the University Hospital when one member underwent serious surgery that when a nurse came on duty and saw the crowd huddled together, she ventured to ask, "What celebrity entered the hospital today?"

STREET PEOPLE AND OTHER UNFORGETTABLE INCIDENTS

During the 1980s, accordion skirts became a popular style. Near the end of one winter season, I found a suit with a blazer-style jacket and an accordion-pleated skirt on sale at one of Birmingham's better department stores and placed it on layaway. By fall, I had it paid for, and proudly wore it to worship the following Sunday. As I walked down the aisle, an older lady hailed my attention.

"Ruby, didn't you know accordion skirts went out of style last year?"

I replied, "That's usually my problem, sister. By the time I have completed payment on my clothing in layaway, it's already gone out of style!" And I continued down the aisle to the front pew.

Joe and I were invited to return to Midway congregation, where he had earlier preached, for a reunion luncheon on a Sunday when Joe was scheduled to preach at a nearby congregation. It caused us to be late for the Midway luncheon. When we arrived, everyone was already seated and dining in the church's huge, long fellowship hall.

Someone at the far end of the hall noticed us enter and remarked, "I wonder who those people are that came in so late."

Another offered, "Oh, it's probably just some street people," and continued eating.

The curious one continued to gaze at us as we came closer and said, "Those people are dressed too well to be street people!"

When they recognized us, they greeted us with much love and, with some embarrassment, related the conversation they had just had about us. We all enjoyed a good laugh.

The second time Joe was invited to serve the Montevallo church for a lengthy engagement, the brethren asked us to spend the entire weekend in their parsonage, which meant we had two properties to manage. It was no easy task, for the unoccupied parsonage had been neglected for some time. We spent many hours making the place habitable and used it for various church gatherings.

One sultry July Saturday afternoon, Joe mowed our lawn before we collected all necessaries for the weekend and hurried to Montevallo. When we arrived, we spent the remainder of the afternoon working in the yard there, mowing, pulling weeds, and pruning shrubs. By late afternoon, our clothes were soiled, our hair disheveled, and both of us were dripping with perspiration.

Suddenly a man walked up and engaged us in conversation, eyeing us closely. It was obvious he had imbibed too much liquor. He told us his daughter lived next door and he was caring for his two grandchildren while she and her husband were away.

Presently, he said, "My daughter told me this house belongs to the minister's family. Are you the caretakers here?"

I answered, "Yes, Sir," knowing that, drunk or sober, no one would ever have believed me if I identified us as the minister's family because of the way we looked.

At one insurance company, Joe's work included collecting weekly premiums in a black neighborhood. He collected mainly from older women who paid for themselves and relatives (or neighbors) who were away at work. As they learned to trust him, that trust turned into fondness, which Joe reciprocated.

They reminded him each week, "Mista, you better git outa heah befo dark cause it ain't safe fuh no white man to be roun heah after dark!"

He appreciated their concern and no problems ever occurred.

Once I accompanied him to Vestavia, a section of Greater Birmingham, when he had an insurance check to deliver. I sat in the car, but I observed clearly what occurred when he knocked on the front door, and the lady of the house answered.

Joe informed her he had a check for her, at which knowledge she grabbed him tightly to herself with all her might and in slurred speech bellowed, "Honey, I've been looking for you! Come on in, and let's have some drinks."

Joe did enter, but he returned to the car momentarily. If he had lingered, I think I could not have helped checking on the two!

One Sunday, while Joe was filling the pulpit at Hoover, there was a young family in the pews for whom he had just completed an interior paint job. As Joe walked toward the pulpit, the family's young son recognized him.

He exclaimed excitedly, "Mama, there goes our painter!"

Another time when Joe was delivering a sermon there, one of the youngsters quizzed his mother as Joe strode toward the podium, "Mama, is that God going there?"

SURPRISE MOVE
(1999-PRESENT)

How we missed our children when they went away to college, later married, and established their own households – all out of state! It left Joe and me in Birmingham with no family, our work and our friends remaining. However, we had trained all of them to become independent, responsible, and self-sufficient adults; in that respect, we were proud of their independence. Life must continue after the nest is empty. Joe continued preaching, along with his secular work; I continued my professional work, along with other random, and sometimes temporary, employment. It included babysitting for a day or a week at a time, interspersed with cooking, cleaning, and sometimes serving as party hostess for two aristocratic families in Birmingham, all of which I relished. In short, we continued working at one thing or another until our move to Crossville, Tennessee.

One day in 1998, Angel surprised us by telephoning, saying she would like for us to move to Crossville where we could live near her. With Starr's family firmly ensconced in Texas and Tony's in California, we knew we could never be near all three of them, as much as we should have liked doing so. However, after recovering from the sudden shock of her proposal, and much prayerful consideration (and, I confess, with some trepidation), we accepted her invitation. Still, we regretted the idea of leaving our work – to say nothing of leaving our dear friends of so many years.

As Joe received no pension from the church, and I received only a small one from BellSouth, we decided one of us would secure part-time employment for several years in our new location, to supplement our modest monthly income. Prior to our move, I applied for teaching positions at Roane State Community College and Tennessee Technical University in Cookeville.

There was much to do: sell our home, close out our work and the organizations in which we were involved. I was in my 10th year as an adjunct instructor at Birmingham's FU. I kept my boss informed of our plans, but he insisted on scheduling me for the summer term of 1999, despite knowing it was possible we could have already moved by then.

The day we closed on the sale of our home, while some of our Christian friends were spending the day helping us pack, the mail brought a letter from Joe's physician. Joe had a malignant tumor in his prostate that needed attention.

After prayerful thought and discussions with a Birmingham urologist, Joe decided we would continue our move as planned and engage a surgeon in Crossville. The Birmingham urologist made the necessary Crossville contacts.

With mixed emotions, we set out for our new home June1, 1999. I cried as we left Birmingham and then shed more tears when we arrived at Angel's house late that afternoon. I suppose it might have been much more emotional, had we waited many more years to make such a significant life change.

Within a few weeks of our move, Joe underwent surgery by a Crossville urologist, who removed the entire prostate; the tumor was so large it pressed against the protective sac that enclosed the prostate.

In the meantime, Joe was called to fill the pulpit at West Avenue, the smaller of two downtown Crossville churches. Following the evening worship, the brethren invited him to be their regular minister. He told them he would be honored to do so, but he was facing surgery and wasn't sure of the outcome. They insisted they were willing to wait for him. Yea! God provides!

The members sent him a custom-made get-well card, which pictured a less-than-handsome dog in a semi-prone position, under which were the words. "You cannot keep a good dog down!"

Joe was hospitalized for a week and was served nothing but yellow Jell-O for the first five days. He joked with his nurses that they had a cunning way of trying to convert him to the Tennessee Volunteers, he, who had been an Alabama Crimson Tide fan for many years. The remaining two days he was hospitalized, he received only green Jell-O! I told him all was well, for one of the colors of my alma mater, UAB, is green.

A few weeks following surgery and consequent radiation treatments, Joe was back in the pulpit for a term that lasted six years, after which he resigned (ostensibly to retire) but was soon filling a need in another pulpit for some years. I began teaching the ladies' class on women of the Bible, a study that lasted seven years, so I jokingly remind Joe occasionally. "I lasted longer at West Avenue than you!"

With that invitation, I was able to decline the offer of an assistant professorship at Tennessee Tech. Both of us were happy that God provided us the opportunity to work locally, enabling us to adjust to the change and become acquainted with people in a setting nearer our new home. We visited in every home in the congregation, save two, and the church grew in number during the six years we served there. Together we conducted many private Bible studies with couples and converted nearly every one of them. All became faithful Christians. Some have gone to their reward already. What a joy to know we have had the privilege of teaching God's word to many along the way!

In addition, Joe assembled a group of Christians, representing several congregations, to form a singing group for funerals. Approximately 20 of us met weekly and practiced *a cappella*. For some six years, we served in that capacity and our singing was so well received, we eventually made a recording, which has been used in funeral homes in Alabama, Florida, Tennessee, and Texas (perhaps in other states, as well). We began to receive invitations to sing for others, among them a cancer group and another church. Some members of the group considered we were performing instead of teaching through song and objected. We considered it a great loss for the entire area when the group disintegrated.

Joe was "retired" only briefly before another need arose with a new congregation. He became their interim minister, for several years. He served as one of the elders for a portion of that time, his third stint in that honorable position, albeit a humbling one of responsibility. In one of the three congregations, he began to understand better the circumstances which ultimately led to the formation of the papacy during the early centuries of the church when one or more church officers practiced superiority over the others of the same rank.

In his permanent retirement, he continues to teach a class and/or fill the pulpit occasionally where there is a temporary need. In addition, he has been called to Birmingham, Cullman, and Montevallo to officiate at funerals of many of our dear friends, and to officiate at weddings for others.

Two other incidents having to do with Joe's ministerial work are distinctive. Our neighbors across the street, Jerry and Carol Swisher, were Catholics. Joe and I were working in our open garage the day Jerry was diagnosed with cancer. Seeing us, he walked over and shared his shocking news. We were sympathetic and lent what encouragement we could.

Jerry had all the attendant treatments, but he suffered – oh, how he suffered! One evening, when Carol was getting ready to attend Mass, Jerry announced he could no longer bear his suffering and he intended to take his own life while she was away. Jerry had earlier received the Sacrament of the Sick (formerly known as Last Rites), but Carol immediately called for a Catholic priest to come. To my knowledge, no priest was available to answer the call.

Another neighbor, who had popped in to check on Jerry and Carol, suggested surely Joe could be of some help – some of our neighbors had already dubbed him as Mountain View Drive's resident minister. She rushed to our house to ask if Joe would go to Jerry and hopefully prevent him from committing suicide.

Joe hurried over; he talked to Jerry, read some scriptures to him, and prayed with him. His intervention resulted in Jerry's abandoning his plan to kill himself.

In the meantime, Jerry's physician ordered stronger dosages of drugs to ease Jerry's pain. All the neighbors extended our love and support in all the ways we could. When he died three months later, Carol asked some of them to participate in Jerry's funeral Mass. She asked Joe to speak some words from the pulpit and follow with a prayer. If we are to believe some of the praise heaped on him, Joe did a superb job of both his remarks and the prayer.

We were invited to a luncheon following the service. Several of the Catholic ladies complimented Joe and asked if he, too, were a minister. When he said, "Yes," they commented, "All our priests have to do to qualify for priesthood is learn to read, but you spoke extemporaneously!" We accepted their comments as a compliment and understood their comments were jokingly made, owing to the fact that Joe's comments were made sans notes, whereas the priests read from their funeral ritual.

Another time, Joe was asked to officiate at the funeral of a Crossville woman who professed to be a Catholic, but had not been attending Mass. A friend of her family asked Joe to conduct the memorial. Joe was always happy to serve in any ministerial capacity, though it is often more difficult to conduct a service of that kind when he knows nothing of the family.

DREAM HOME

Long before I met Joe, he had begun collecting books. Once I began collecting, together we possessed a library of more than 3,000 volumes after having given away a few hundred of them. When we decided to move to Crossville, we searched for a house with a library sufficient to house our collection. Finding none, it eventually occurred to us to build a house and construct a library in it.

For many years I had collected ideas for building a house suited to our lifestyle. We perused all my notes and pictures, made a plan, and purchased a lot at 120 Mountain View Drive in Fairfield Glade. Our efforts congealed into specific requirements. The house should have only one floor with three divisions: on one side a library, master bedroom with separate walk-in closets, and a large bathroom with dual vanities; the middle portion should have a large open area serving as a foyer, a formal dining room, a large living room/den with fireplace, and a kitchen/breakfast area separated from the living room by a partial wall, with columns placed throughout to distinguish each area; the opposite side of the house should contain two guest bedrooms separated by a bathroom. A hallway toward the middle of the house led to all three areas.

We had owned homes in Birmingham and remodeled one of them, but I was lost, trying to build a new house, as I admit total ignorance of building terms. In addition, it took a great deal of redesigning with our contractor to build the house according to our specifications. It was a stressful nine months' undertaking, though the contractor had promised to be finished in only three! Meantime, we rented a small house and left most of our possessions stored.

I worked diligently to coordinate colors throughout the house and made nearly every accessory, curtains, pillows, throws (afghans), table runners and table linens. Starr came one week and helped with sewing some of the curtains. On our long, L-shaped hall, I hung prized family portraits. Later, when I began oil painting, I mounted many pieces of my art work on appropriate wall areas.

Building the house. and all the things associated with it, was stressful for me, but Joe and I were pleased with the finished product. In our open area we could seat 18, counting the breakfast area…and we often did, for I wished to continue to invite people into our home for meals.

The house remained our dream home for 17 years, until failing health demanded we have help or downsize. Downsizing it became. That, too, was stressful, as it necessitated our parting with so much of our accumulation of 60+ years.

A New Hobby

Virtually all my life I had sewn for myself, my daughters, and others, and created many gifts as well. I won first place on a dress I submitted at the Shelby County, Alabama, fair one year. (The second-place winner was a woman who sewed professionally.) At age 55, I received one crocheting lesson from Mother, determined to carry on what she had established as a family tradition. I won first place on a crocheted top in state competition, submitted through a DAR Heritage Arts contest a few years ago.

I met artist Helen Holladay soon after we moved to Crossville; she was in the room adjoining Joe's when both were recovering from surgery. I paid Helen a visit, which she obviously did not forget, for when I met her downtown some time later, she invited me to become a student in her art class. I declined because I had never dreamed of painting, though I'd often admired fine art work. Helen insisted, every time we met thereafter, I must become her student. I persistently refused. Then one day I mentioned Helen's invitation to Starr, who convinced me I should at least try my hand. How could I know whether I had any inclination in that direction as long as I refused to make any attempt?

Reluctantly I began, and with her instructions, on the mark for her though difficult for me, I have produced work of which I am quite proud (some of which I have even sold). I also frequently frame my work as gifts.

I have painted birds and animals – including my niece's favorite cat, Sophie – and Tony's dog, Marlow, which we kept once for 14 months while Tony was abroad on a work assignment. Other painting subjects have included the tenant farmhouse in which I was born; the one-room school house where I attended grammar school; the Cane Ridge Meeting House in Kentucky, where many religious groups gathered for Bible study from the late 1700s to early 1800s, as they were unhappy with their church's teaching; the house of worship at Gladeville, and many pictures of flowers.

Continued suffering from serious injuries to both knees and from a tick bite, which impaired my body from head to toe, has forced me to take a hiatus from painting. Helen is a tremendous artist, and all of us who painted together are good friends; I trust we shall remain friends, regardless of whether I am ever able to make any artist's brush strokes again.

OTHER ACTIVITIES

In 2011, I organized an informal book club on our street. Each member takes a turn hosting the club in her home and providing refreshments before presenting a summary of her chosen book, followed by a period of discussion. No one is required to read the work in advance, but usually some are inspired to read the book afterward. We are concluding our seventh year of ten monthly meetings per year. We have learned much from each other and have established stronger bonds of friendship.

Also, I have spent a great deal of time documenting some of my ancestral lines. I learned my paternal GGG grandfather. William Yates of Raleigh, North Carolina, served in the Revolutionary War; his son, my GG grandfather, Alsey Yates, also of Raleigh, fought in the War of 1812; Alsey's son, Ruffin Yates of Gibson County, Tennessee, was my great-grandfather. My grandfather, Raleigh Parker Yates, lived with him for an entire year following the death of his wife, Beulah J. (Lowrance) Yates, along with some of his children, my father included, until Grandfather remarried, this time to a Foster maid. When she died some years later, Grandfather married a third time to his second wife's sister, also a maid. Amazingly enough, Grandfather Yates outlived all three wives!

On my maternal side, I learned James M. Green of Warren/DeKalb County, Tennessee, was the father of Mary Ann Green, who became my mother's grandmother, making him my great-great grandfather. Green volunteered to serve in the Confederate Army at age 39, re-enlisting at age 40 after he was sent home (because the legal age of draftees at that time was 18 to 35 years). On the day of his first enlistment, he submitted to the rite of baptism, so I assume he took his undertaking seriously. I might add he was a successful farmer *sans* slaves – he fought for his "country" – and a pre-Civil War school in his community at the time bears the name Green School, leading me to believe he was at the very least involved in it, for his handwriting is beautiful and legible, whereas so many Southerners were illiterate at that time.

I uncovered additional history about Grandfather Green. He was a savvy entrepreneur, for he purchased land, improved it, and sold it at a profit. According to the record of the estate sale following his death in 1900, he had lent money to many people.

Once I located GG Grandfather Green's tombstone, I cleaned it and could see the design on it indicated he was a member of the Woodmen of the World, founded in 1890, making him a member during its first decade of existence. Since I could not uncover a specific member number to identify him, the headquarters of the Woodmen refused to put forth any effort to locate his records in their files.

I planned a memorial service for him on site in 2014 with approximately 40 in attendance, including several cousins and two nieces. Angel placed flowers on his grave, and grandson Aaron Ingram sang some hymns that would have been popular during the Victorian era. I presented a brief history of him gleaned from various sources. The Sons of Confederate Veterans (SCV) placed a Confederate stone at the base of his monument.

Having learned a great deal about my ancestral background, I became eligible for membership in several historical organizations, including the Daughters of the American Revolution (DAR), and the U.S. Daughters of 1812. I also established the Tennessee Society of the Order of Confederate Rose (OCR), which exists to support the SCV. I have served in various capacities in all these organizations and continue as an active member of all of them. I currently serve as chaplain of both the DAR and the U.S. Daughters of 1812.

Joe and Angel have given me great joy, both of them having been members of the Cumberland County Community Chorus in Crossville, performing several concerts in the spring and in the fall (only after having spent 12 weekly practice sessions and training for each season's concerts). For a few years Joe was also a member of the Festival Chorale, which had the privilege of performing at Carnegie Hall. Angel, Starr, and I attended the concert. For the event, we managed to piece together a complete ensemble for Joe – at a thrifty price.

Our next-door neighbors, Dennis and Carolyn Merrill, surprised us with the gift of a beautiful woolen gabardine tuxedo, part of Dennis' wedding ensemble, which remained in perfect condition, but no longer fit Dennis. A gift certificate Angel and Starr had given their father went toward the purchase of a tuxedo shirt, cummerbund, bow tie, studs, and cuff links. We were delighted to spy a window display of men's used patent leather shoes in Crossville's Vanity Fair Mall and purchased a pair for the bargain price of $22. They were in excellent condition and a perfect fit. (Their thick soles stood Joe in good stead through the long hours of practice, once the chorus arrived in New York, and for the length of the concert, as well.) There remained only one thing to complete his ensemble: a pair of black dress socks. I searched unsuccessfully in local department stores and was pleased finally to find a new pair in one of Crossville's second-hand stores – for 50 cents!

I remarked to Joe, "New York, we are ready, and here we come!"

Joe later admitted he'd secreted a pair of his everyday black cotton socks into his luggage and wore them with his tuxedo ensemble, instead of the dress socks I was such a long time in finding.

NEW WORK AND
NEW FRIENDS

The first Sunday Joe preached at West Avenue, two lovely widows, Charlene Bailey and Margaret Jones, sisters in the flesh as well as in God's family, took us out to lunch. Both were older than I, but Charlene and I bonded especially quickly and became fast friends. We did many things together. I sometimes drove her to Chattanooga for checkups with her heart specialist. We shared meals in each other's homes. Often, she prepared a cake, deviled eggs, and potato salad and brought them when she knew any of our children was due to visit. We worked Bible quizzes and Bible puzzles independently, then compared our answers. We spoke regularly on the telephone.

One other fine Christian sister at West Avenue, Cleda Eller, and I bonded belatedly. Cleda told me later she "waited to be sure I was okay" before she lent her close friendship. We sometimes drove to Muddy Pond, home to Mennonites, where we purchased their homemade or custom-made items. Cleda saved all her bacon drippings for me to use in soap making. In return, I shared some of my soap with her. I also donated items for her twice-yearly garage sales and went by to purchase a few things from her. She used her profits to purchase ingredients to make delicious candy and cookies to give at Christmas time. Hundreds of people in Crossville were annual recipients of her homemade goodies – Joe and I among them – all of which required many days of Cleda's labor-intensive work.

Both Charlene and Cleda have now gone on to their reward. Long before her death, Charlene asked Joe to participate in her funeral service and specified which of our recorded funeral hymns she wanted played. I was privileged to launder and press her burial clothing, a beautiful white gown with delicate pink roses embroidered on the collar and cuffs of the long sleeves, a perfect match for the roses embroidered inside her casket.

Though I have made other friends here and at other places, none surpasses the love and joy with which those two friends enriched my life. I'll carry their memory to the grave with me.

OTHER ACCIDENTS
AND ILLNESS

The back lawn of our Mountain View Drive home was bordered by an all-wooded area, which altogether composed 136 acres, full of coyotes, deer, foxes, and turkeys, perhaps other animals – even bears have been spotted. Many of those animals bore ticks, some of which carried poisonous bacteria.

As the gardener in our household, I was frequently cleaning flower beds and pulling weeds. I have pulled many ticks from my body without consequence; but one disease-carrying tick – hidden beneath the fold of my right breast – went undiscovered for several days and came close to costing my life. When I discovered it, there was an angry-looking, fiery-red swollen bull's eye surrounding the tick.

When Joe attempted to remove the tick, it burst. I immediately went to a walk-in clinic where the physician on duty excised the remainder of it and prescribed a typical 10-day course of doxycycline. Had I known to ask that the tick be analyzed, it might have prevented years of suffering and bodily impairment, not to mention expense.

Within a few days, a rash began at the site of the affected area, and I became deathly sick with swooshing fluid in my head and in my ears; a stiff neck; arthritic symptoms in my shoulders, back, hips, among other parts; and severe pain in my right foot made a cripple of me. A bone in one of the toes on my left foot actually popped into as I exited the doctor's office one afternoon. No doctor in this area seemed inclined to help me, though I tried to convince several I was suffering from a tick infection. All of them said one did not get Lyme disease in this part of Tennessee. Later years have proven them wrong, for others in this area have been infected seriously enough to require hospitalization.

I suffered for six months before I learned of a tick specialist in Springfield, Missouri, and became his patient. Unfortunately, he said there was no curing me after having been infected so broadly for such an extended period of time, but he hoped to help me manage it. I was under his care for 18 months, during which time I took six different kinds of powerful drugs, each for an extended period. I required various other medicines to counter the effect of each powerful drug.

After a year and a half, I found a physician in Crossville who agreed to care for me, so I became her patient for several more months. She not only prescribed medications but administered treatments designed to clean my blood of impurities. My condition gradually improved, but many parts of my body continue to bear the effects of the disease.

Later, I crushed my right kneecap and sustained other damage in a fall on concrete, rekindling the pain from my long-ago basketball injury. Another similar fall injured my other knee. Each time, I was compelled to use a walker for an extended period, but finally healed sufficiently to walk again – albeit with a limp. I have never fully recovered, and suffer pain daily, despite a complete replacement of my right knee.

EVENING ARRIVES

After 17 years in our custom-built house, age and infirmity forced us to downsize. We had no difficulty selling our house – the first ones to view it purchased it. Ridding ourselves of possessions collected over our 63 years of marriage was painful, I must admit, though perhaps it shouldn't have been, for they are just things. We kept minimal furnishings, sold a few others, gave the children some items, and hauled six loads of miscellaneous household goods, clothing, etc., to benevolent organizations.

We purchased the middle unit of a small triplex, too small even to house the few clothes and scant furnishings we kept. Still, we did our best to adjust to our reduced circumstances.

One Sunday morning in October 2016 our house was burglarized while we were in worship. Though we lost many items dear to us, the thieves did not collect all they might have, for a friend drove up and parked in front of our unit about 15 minutes before we arrived home. Upon examination, it became obvious (from the broken curtain rod on the partially opened back door) the intruders rushed out the back door when they saw our friend's vehicle out front and escaped into the adjoining woods.

A few weeks later, there was a second attempt at forced entry. Fortunately, someone thwarted the thieves' efforts and no additional items were lost. After that second unsettling incident, I told Joe I could never feel safe there anymore, as much as I dreaded the thought of another move – our second in a little over a year. The only comfort was we had fewer possessions to move this time around.

We felt God's guiding hand once again, for Joe found a duplex in a development just outside Fairfield Glade, which provides for our current needs. We were able to purchase it and sell our other property. We've had to buy a few secondhand pieces of furniture, but we are settling in nicely as I write; I pray we can live out the remainder of our days with no additional moves. When people ask why we moved twice in such a short time, my answer is, "Because we are gypsies!"

AFTERWORD

In the evening of my life, I remain as active every day as my health permits. I write a brief weekly religious article published in two local papers and teach a ladies' Bible class occasionally. In addition to housework and hosting meals, I am active in the book club I started seven years ago and am regularly involved in charitable activities, in addition to assisting in the good works of the historical organizations to which I belong.

Also, in April 2017, I was invited to conduct a Ladies' Day for the Columbiana, Alabama, congregation, where Joe and I served during the late 1970s and 1980s. (Our hosts, Richard and Beth Glasgow, allowed us to enjoy an extended stay in their lake house on a cove of the Coosa River. It was in that peaceful setting I composed a portion of my life story.) Many whom I had known during our Birmingham years flocked to the Ladies' Day event. I have heard it said if people still love you once they know you well, you have true friends...and many of those in attendance knew me quite well! In addition to the Columbiana sisters and others from neighboring congregations, there were former colleagues from BellSouth, former neighbors, my hairdresser of many years, Telephone Pioneer friends, local visitors, and various others. It was a joyous and uplifting reunion I shall cherish the remainder of my life.

As I reflect on my life, I feel extremely fortunate for the multitudinous ways God has blessed me. I chose what Robert Frost calls "the road less traveled," and it has, indeed, made all the difference. I do not claim to have achieved fame, for that was never my goal. Yet I persevered and consider it a worthwhile accomplishment to have overcome shyness, dire poverty, and the mental, physical, and sexual abuse to which I was subjected as a child and reached a certain level of success, though I have no thought of comparing myself with those who are truly great. At the least, rearing a godly family in an ungodly world is no little accomplishment for anyone. I am the daughter of *The Noble Orphan.*

www.ingramcontent.com/pod-product-compliance
Lightning Source LLC
Chambersburg PA
CBHW021622120626
46545CB00001B/360